Rich Dad's

INCREASE YOUR
FINANCIAL
IQ

INCREASE YOUR FINANCIAL IQ

Get Smarter with Your Money

By Robert T. Kiyosaki

Special Thanks to **Jake Johnson**
for collaborative editorial work

BUSINESS PLUS

NEW YORK   BOSTON

Originally published in trade paperback by Hachette Book Group
First international mass market edition: May 2009

Quotations from the following sources appear in this book:

Eleanor Laise, "What Is Your 401(k) Costing You?" *Wall Street Journal*, March 14, 2007.
Justin Lahart, "How the 'Quant' Playbook Failed," *Wall Street Journal*, August 24, 2007.

CASHFLOW, Rich Dad, Rich Dad's Advisors, Rich Dad's Seminars, EBSI, B-I Triangle are registered trademarks of CASHFLOW Technologies, Inc.

Business Plus
Hachette Book Group
237 Park Avenue
New York, NY 10017

Visit our Web sites at www.HachetteBookGroup.com and www.richdad.com.

Business Plus is an imprint of Grand Central Publishing.
The Business Plus name and logo are trademarks of Hachette Book Group, Inc.

Printed in the United States of America

10 9 8 7 6 5 4 3 2 1

Contents

Foreword: A Capitalist's Point of View on Education

We are experiencing one of the worst financial crises in our country's history—a crisis that has the potential to affect not only ourselves, but also our children's children. It cannot be stressed enough that what we are facing in today's economic upheaval is not just a disruption of credit, but a crisis for the very soul of capitalism. As Saint Bernard of Clairvaux would warn us, "Hell is full of good intentions or desires." And unfortunately, today in America, good intention has all but replaced informed decisions. This is no more apparent than in looking at the terrifying naiveté with which our so-called leaders are addressing the current economic emergency. As a consequence, many of us will suffer because of what our government and business leaders have done both to cause and to further this economic emergency and by their attempts to repair the damage.

It's truly a tragedy that the hard work accomplished by courageous leaders such as Ronald Reagan to strengthen the dollar and open wide the channels of free-market capitalism are now being cast away by politicians and bureaucrats who are more concerned with pandering than leading. Already the roads of capitalism and free markets have been washed out by a wave of socialistic claptrapping. The U.S. government now effectively owns the largest mortgage providers in the nation as well as the largest insurer in the nation, and it will soon own large stakes in desperate corporations that have little choice but to sell their subprime assets to the government thanks to ridiculous regulatory requirements such as mark to market (MTM).

But a bigger tragedy than the credit crisis, or even the degradation of a capitalist system that has brought such prosperity to the American people, is that so few of us truly understand what happened, and even more so, why it happened; nor do we understand what we should do to protect ourselves and our economy. And because many of us don't understand these things, many of the opportunities that face us today will slip through our fingers, and many of the challenges we face will continue for a long time. The ability of many people to realize the American Dream—admirably defined by Abraham Lincoln, who said that every American should have the opportunity to "improve his lot in life"—is severely inhibited by our country's severe lack of financial education. As the prophet Hosea put it so eloquently, "My people perish for lack of knowledge."

So, what's the solution? By what means can we reclaim the diminished soul of capitalism? What measures must be taken to avoid our economic perishing? The answer, like so many wise and effective solutions, is simple: education. It is education alone that provides the knowledge necessary to remove barriers to opportunity. For by education we move past the limiting bonds of good intention and embrace an effective and informed pragmatism that only knowledge and understanding can bring.

For many people the key to abundant life and enjoying financial security is to understand the system and how to make it work for them—to gain financial intelligence and, as Robert puts it so well, to increase their financial IQ. This is a lifelong process. You don't have to be a genius to take part in this process; you simply have to be ready, willing, and able to learn.

Practical, applicable knowledge of finance and economics is not pass/fail. It's not a case of you either know it or you don't. It's a reciprocal process of learning and applying knowledge about money, finance, and economics, and how those things, and the ways in which you respond to and act on them, impact your daily life. The more you know, the better equipped you are to prosper. The higher your financial IQ, the stronger your financial performance will be.

Financial education isn't just numbers and spreadsheets, although they're certainly a part of it. Financial education requires a solid understanding of how business and government work (or don't work as the case may be). And it's also knowing about history, humanities and human nature, arts and science, and music and mechanics, among other things. To be a whole, healthy, and well-equipped citizen requires a holistic education that focuses not just on numbers and spreadsheets but also on the soul itself.

All education has value, and all education can be useful as you discover and fully develop your own God-given talents. As an advocate of democratic capitalism, I believe education is critical to the economic well-being of our country and is vital to continuing America's role as a shining beacon in a world that is often dark. Education is vitally necessary if people are to realize their full potential, and it's absolutely essential if individuals are to take responsibility for their own circumstances and thrive in the economic maelstrom in which we find ourselves.

This is why I applaud Robert Kiyosaki's efforts to bring financial education to people who want to change their lives, achieve financial security, and develop the resources to live the life of their dreams. That you're reading this excellent book means you're on the right track to bettering yourself and your country. That is why I also applaud you. Enjoy this book—I know I have—and may it be another part of a life-long process of gaining knowledge and understanding.

—Steve Forbes

Foreword

I first met Robert Kiyosaki in 2004. We wrote a bestselling book together in 2006. As we head into 2008, it's become even clearer to me that what Robert talks about and teaches is more important than ever. Financial education is crucial to this country at this point, and Robert's acumen in this area cannot be disputed.

Just look at what was discussed in our book, *Why We Want You To Be Rich,* and then take a look at what has happened since then. I'd say we knew what we were talking about. Robert is taking you one step further with *Rich Dad's Increase Your Financial IQ* and I have every reason to believe he will be as prescient as we were in 2006. I would advise you to pay attention to what he has to say.

Robert and I have shared concerns and we have traveled similar paths as teachers and businessmen. Both of us had rich dads who helped to shape our lives, our spirits, and our many successes. We are both entrepreneurs and real estate investors, and we are successful because we had financial education. We know its importance and are serious when it comes to financial literacy. Robert has said, "It's financial education that enables people to process financial information and turn it into knowledge . . . and most people don't have the financial education they need to take charge of their lives." I couldn't agree more.

One thing I noticed immediately about Robert is that he is not complacent. He's very successful already—because he loves what he's doing. That's another thing we have in common. That's fortunate for you, because he has a lot of very good advice to give. As I said in *Why We Want You To Be Rich*, what's the point of having great knowledge and keeping it to yourself? Robert answers that question with every book he writes, and you're lucky he's sharing it with you.

One of the first steps to getting richer by getting smarter with your money is to take advantage of opportunities when they present themselves. Right now you are holding a great opportunity. My advice to you is to read *Rich Dad's Increase Your Financial IQ* and to pay attention. You will be on the right path to financial freedom, and on the right path to big success. By the way, don't forget to Think Big. We'll see you in the winner's circle.

—Donald J. Trump

Author's Note

Money Is Not Evil

One of the greatest failures of the educational system is the failure to provide financial education to students. Educators seem to think that money has some sort of quasi-religious or cultlike taint to it, believing *that the love of money is the root of all evil.*

As most of us know, it is not the love of money that is evil—it is the lack of money that causes evil. It is working at a job we hate that is evil. Working hard yet not earning enough to provide for our families is evil. For some, being deeply in debt is evil. Fighting with people you love over money is evil. Being greedy is evil. And committing criminal or immoral acts to get money is evil. Money by itself is not evil. Money is just money.

Your House Is Not an Asset

The lack of financial education also causes people to do stupid things or be misled by stupid people. For example, in 1997, when I first published *Rich Dad Poor Dad* and stated that "Your house is not an asset . . . your house is a liability," howls of protest went up. My book and I were severely criticized. Many self-proclaimed financial experts attacked me in the media. Ten years later, in 2007, as the credit markets crumbled and millions of people were in financial free fall—many losing their homes, some declaring bankruptcy, others owing more on their house than it was worth as real estate dropped in value—these individuals painfully found out that their homes *are indeed liabilities*, not assets.

Two Men, One Message

In 2006, my friend Donald Trump and I wrote a book entitled *Why We Want You To Be Rich*. We wrote about why the middle class was falling behind and what we thought the causes of the decline were. We said that many of the causes were in the global, government, and financial markets. This book was also attacked by the financial media. But by 2007, most of what we said had come true.

Obsolete Advice

Today, many financial experts continue to recommend, "Work hard, save money, get out of debt, live below your means, and invest in a well-diversified portfolio of mutual funds." The problem with this advice is that it is *bad advice*—simply because it is *obsolete advice*. The rules of money have changed. They changed in 1971. Today there is a new capitalism. Saving money, getting out of debt, and diversifying worked in the era of old capitalism. Those who follow the "work hard and save money" mantra of *old capitalism* will struggle financially in the era of *new capitalism*.

Information vs. Education

It is this author's opinion that the lack of financial education in our school systems is a cruel and evil shame. In today's world, financial education is absolutely essential for survival, regardless of whether we are rich or poor, smart or not smart.

As most of us know, we now live in the Information Age. The problem with the Information Age is *information overload*. Today, there is too much information. The equation below explains why financial education is so important.

Information + Education = Knowledge

Without financial education, people cannot process information into useful knowledge. Without financial knowledge, people struggle financially. Without financial knowledge, people do things such as buy a house and think their home is an asset. Or save money, not realizing that since 1971, their money is no longer money but a currency. Or do not know the difference between good debt and bad debt. Or why the rich earn more yet pay less in taxes. Or why the richest investor in the world, Warren Buffett, does not diversify.

Leaping Lemmings

Without financial knowledge, people look for someone to tell them what to do. And what most financial experts recommend is to work hard, save money, get out of debt, live below your means, and invest in a well-diversified portfolio of mutual funds. Like lemmings simply following their leader, they race for the cliff and leap into the ocean of financial uncertainty hoping they can swim to the other side.

This Book Is Not about Financial Advice

This book will not tell you what to do. This book is not about financial advice. This book is about your becoming financially smarter so you can process your own financial information and find your own path to financial nirvana.

In sum, this book is about becoming richer by becoming smarter. This book is about increasing your financial IQ.

Introduction

Does Money Make You Rich?

It is well enough that people of the nation do not understand our banking and monetary system, for if they did, I believe there would be a revolution before tomorrow morning.

—HENRY FORD

The answer is *No*. Money alone does not make you rich. We all know people who go to work every day, working for money, making more money, but fail to become richer. Ironically, many only grow deeper in debt with each dollar they earn. We have all heard stories of lottery winners, instant millionaires, who are instantly poor again. We have also heard stories of real estate going into foreclosure. Instead of making homeowners richer, more financially secure, real estate drives homeowners out of their homes and into the poorhouse. Many of us know of individuals who have lost money investing in the stock market. Maybe you are one of those individuals. Even investing in gold—the world's only real money— can cost the investor money.

Gold was my first real investment as a young adult. I began investing in gold before I began investing in real estate. In 1972, at the age of twenty-five, I began buying gold coins when gold was approximately $70 an ounce. By 1980, gold was approaching $800 an ounce. The frenzy was on. Greed overtook caution. Rumors were that gold was going to hit $2,500 an ounce. Greedy investors began piling on, buying gold, even though they had never done so before. But instead of selling some of my gold coins and making a small profit, I hung on, also hoping that gold would go higher. About a year later, as gold dropped below $500 an ounce, I finally sold my last coin. From 1980, I watched as gold drifted lower and lower till it finally bottomed out at $250 in 1999.

Although I did not make much money, gold taught me many priceless lessons about money. Once I realized that I could lose money investing in real money, gold, I realized that it was not gold, the asset, that was valuable. It was the *information* relative to the asset that ultimately made a person rich or poor. In other words, *it is not real estate, stocks, mutual funds, businesses, or money that makes a person rich. It is information, knowledge, wisdom, and know-how, a.k.a. financial intelligence, that makes one wealthy.*

Golf Lessons or Golf Clubs

A friend of mine is a golfing fanatic. He spends thousands of dollars a year on new clubs and every new golf gadget that comes to market. The problem is, he will not spend a dime on golf lessons. Hence his golf game remains the same, even though he has the latest and greatest in golf equipment. If he invested his money in golf lessons and used last year's clubs, he might be a much better golfer.

The same nutty phenomenon occurs in the game of money. Billions of people invest their hard-earned money in assets such as stocks and real estate, but invest almost nothing in information. Hence their financial scores remain about the same.

Not a Magic Formula

This book is not a get-rich-quick book or a book about some magic formula. This book is about increasing your financial intelligence, your financial IQ. It is about getting richer by getting smarter. It is about *the five basic financial intelligences* that are required to grow richer, regardless of what the economy, stocks, or real estate markets are doing.

The New Rules of Money

This book is also about the new rules of money, rules that changed in 1971. It is because of these changes in the rules that the old rules are obsolete. One of the reasons why so many people are struggling financially is because they continue to operate according to the old rules of money, old rules such as *work hard, save money, get out of debt, invest for the long term in a well-diversified portfolio of stocks, bonds, and mutual funds*. This book is about playing by the new rules of money, but to do so requires increasing your financial intelligence and your financial IQ.

After reading this book, you will be better able to determine if it is better for you to play by the *old rules* or the *new rules* of money.

Finding Your Financial Genius

Chapter nine of this book is about finding your financial genius by utilizing all three parts of your brain. As most of us know, the three parts of our brain are the left, right, and subconscious brain.

The reason most people do not become rich is because the subconscious brain is the most powerful of the three parts. For example, people may study real estate and know exactly what to do via their left and right brains, but the powerful subconscious part of their brains can take control, saying, "Oh, that's too risky. What if you lose your money? What if you make a mistake?" In this example, the emotion of fear is causing the subconscious brain to work against the desires of the left and right brain. Simply said, to develop your financial genius it is important to first know how to get all three parts of your brain to work in harmony rather than against each other. This book will explain how you can do that.

In Short

Many people believe that it takes money to make money. This is not true. Always remember that if you can lose money investing in gold, you can lose money in anything. Ultimately, it is not gold, stocks, real estate, hard work, or money that makes you rich—*it is what you know* about gold, stocks, real estate, hard work, and money that makes you rich. Ultimately, it is your financial intelligence, your financial IQ, that makes you rich.

Please read on and become richer by becoming smarter.

Chapter 1

What Is Financial Intelligence?

When I was five years old, I was rushed to the hospital for emergency surgery. As I understand it, I had a serious infection in my ears, a complication from chicken pox. Although it was a frightening experience, I have a cherished memory of my dad, my younger brother, and my two sisters standing on the lawn outside the hospital window waving to me as I lay in bed recovering. My mom was not there. She was at home, bedridden, struggling with a weak heart.

Within a year, my younger brother was taken to the hospital after falling from a ledge in the garage and landing on his head. My younger sister was next. She needed an operation on her knee. And the youngest, my sister Beth, a newborn baby, had a severe skin disorder that continually baffled the doctors.

It was a tough year for my dad, and he was the only one out of six not to succumb to a medical challenge. The good news is that we all recovered and lived healthy lives. The bad news was the medical bills that kept coming. My father may not have become ill that year, but he did contract a crippling malady—overwhelming medical debt.

At the time, my dad was a graduate student at the University of Hawaii. He was brilliant in school, receiving his bachelor's degree in just two years, and had dreams of one day becoming a college professor. Now with a family of six, a mortgage, and high medical bills to pay, he let go of his dream and took a job as an assistant superintendent of schools in the little town of Hilo, on the Big Island of Hawaii. Just so he could afford to move our family from one island to another he had to get a loan from his own father. It was a tough time for him and for our family.

Although he did achieve tremendous professional success and was finally awarded his doctorate degree, I suspect not realizing his dream of becoming a college professor haunted my father until his dying days. He often said, "When you kids are out of the house, I'm going back to school and doing what I love—teaching."

Instead of teach, however, he eventually became the superintendent of education for the state of Hawaii, an administrative post, and then ran for lieutenant governor and lost. At the age of fifty, he was suddenly unemployed. Soon after the election, my mom suddenly died at the age of forty-eight due to her weak heart. My father never recovered from that loss.

Once again, money problems piled up. Without a job, he decided to withdraw his retirement savings, and invested in a national ice-cream franchise. He lost all his money.

As he grew older my father felt he was left behind by his peers; his life's career was over. Without his job as the head of education, his identity was gone. He grew angrier at his rich classmates who had gone into business, rather than education as he did. Lashing out, he often said, "I dedicated my life to educating the children of Hawaii, and what do I get? Nothing. My fat-cat classmates get richer, and what do I get? Nothing."

I will never know why he did not go back to the university to teach. I believe it was because he was trying very hard to become rich quickly and to make up for lost time. He wound up chasing flakey deals and hanging out with fast-talking con men. None of his get-rich-quick ventures succeeded.

If not for a few odd jobs and Social Security, he might have had to move in with one of the kids. A few months before he died of cancer at the age of seventy-two, my father pulled me close to his bedside and apologized for not having much to leave his children. Holding his hand, I put my head on his hand and we cried together.

Not Enough Money

My poor dad had money problems all his life. No matter how much money he made, his problem was *not enough money*. His inability to solve that problem caused him great pain up till he died. Tragically, he felt inadequate, both professionally and as a father.

Being from the world of academics, he did his best to push his financial problems aside and dedicate his life to a higher cause than money. He did his best to assert that money did not matter, even when it did. He was a great man, a great husband and father, and a brilliant educator; yet it was this thing called money that often called the shots, silently hounded him, and, sadly, towards the end, was the measure he used to evaluate his life. As smart as he was, he never solved his money problems.

Too Much Money

My rich dad, who began to teach me about money at the age of nine, also had money problems. He solved his money problems differently than my poor dad. He acknowledged that money did matter, and because he realized that, he strove to increase his financial intelligence at every chance. To him that meant tackling his money problems head-on and learning from the process. My rich dad was not nearly as academically smart as my poor dad, but because he solved his money problems differently, and increased his financial intelligence, my rich dad's money problem was *too much money*.

Having two dads, one rich and one poor, I learned that rich or poor, we all have money problems.

The money problems of the poor are:

1. Not having enough money.
2. Using credit to supplement money shortages.
3. The rising cost of living.
4. Paying more in taxes the more they make.
5. Fear of emergencies.
6. Bad financial advice.
7. Not enough retirement money.

The money problems of the rich are:

1. Having too much money.
2. Needing to keep it safe and invested.
3. Not knowing whether people like them, or their money.
4. Needing smarter financial advisors.
5. Raising spoiled kids.
6. Estate and inheritance planning.
7. Excessive government taxes.

My poor dad had money problems all his life. No matter how much money he made, his problem was *not enough money*. My rich dad also had money problems. His problem was *too much money*. Which money problem do you want?

Poor Solutions to Money Problems

Learning at an early age that we all have money problems, no matter how rich or how poor we are, was a very important lesson for me. Many people believe that if they had a lot of money, their money problems would be over. Little do they know that having lots of money just causes even more money problems.

One of my favorite commercials is for a financial services company and starts with the rapper MC Hammer dancing with beautiful women, a Bentley and a Ferrari and a grossly oversized mansion behind him. In the background, high-end specialty goods are being moved into the mansion. MC Hammer's one-hit wonder, "U Can't Touch This," is playing as all this is happening. Then the screen goes black and displays the words "15 minutes later." The next scene is MC Hammer sitting on a curb in front of the same ridiculous mansion, his head in his hands, next to a sign that reads "FORECLOSED." The announcer says, "Life comes at you fast. We're here to help."

The world is full of MC Hammers. We all have heard of lottery winners who win millions and then are deeply in debt a few years later. Or the young professional athlete who lives in a mansion while he is playing and then lives under a bridge once his playing days are over. Or the young rock star who is a multimillionaire in his twenties and looking for a job in his thirties. (Or the rapper who is peddling financial services that he was probably *already* using when he lost his money.)

Money alone does not solve your money problems. That is why giving poor people money does not solve their money problems. In many cases, it only prolongs the problem and creates more poor people. Take for instance the idea of welfare. From the time of the Great Depression until 1996, the government guaranteed money to the nation's poor regardless of personal circumstance. All you had to do was qualify for the poverty requirements to receive a government check—perpetually. If you showed initiative, got a job, and earned more than the poverty requirement, the government cut off your benefits. Of course, the poor then had other costs associated with working that they didn't have before, such as uniforms, child care, transportation, etc. In many cases they ended up with less money than before they had a job, and less time. The system benefited those who were lazy and punished those who showed initiative. The system created more poor people.

Hard work doesn't solve money problems. The world is filled with hardworking people who have no money to show for it, hardworking people who earn money, yet grow deeper in debt, needing to work even harder for even more money.

Education does not solve money problems. The world is filled with highly educated poor people. They're called socialists.

A job does not solve money problems. For many people, the letters J.O.B. stand for *just over broke.* There are millions who earn just enough to survive but cannot afford to live. Many people with jobs cannot afford their own home, adequate health care, education, or even set aside enough money for retirement.

What Solves Money Problems?

Financial intelligence solves money problems. In simple terms, financial intelligence is that part of our total intelligence we use to solve financial problems. Some examples of very common money problems are:

1. "I don't earn enough money."
2. "I'm deeply in debt."
3. "I can't afford to buy a home."
4. "My car is broken. How do I find the money to fix it?"

5. "I have $10,000. What should I invest in?"
6. "My child wants to go to college, but we don't have the money."
7. "I don't have enough money for retirement."
8. "I don't like my job, but I can't afford to quit."
9. "I'm retired, and I'm running out of money."
10. "I can't afford the surgery."

Financial intelligence solves these and other money problems. Unfortunately, if our financial intelligence is not developed enough to solve our problems, the problems persist. They don't go away. Many times they get worse, causing even more money problems. For example, there are millions of people who do not have enough money set aside for retirement. If they fail to solve that problem, the problem will get worse, as they grow older and require more money for medical care. Like it or not, money does affect lifestyle and quality of life—as well as afford conveniences and hassle-free choices. The freedom of choice that money offers can mean the difference between hitchhiking or taking the bus . . . or traveling by private jet.

Solving Money Problems Makes You Smarter
When I was a young boy, rich dad said to me, "Money problems make you smarter . . . if you solve the problem." He also said, "If you solve your money problem, your financial intelligence grows. When your financial intelligence grows, you become richer. If you *do not* solve your money problem, you become poorer. If you do not solve your money problem, that problem often grows into more problems." If you want to increase your financial intelligence, you need to be a problem-solver. If you don't solve your money problems you will never be rich. In fact, you will become poorer the longer the problem persists.

Rich dad used the example of having a toothache to illustrate what he meant by a problem leading to other problems. He said, "Having a money problem is like having a toothache. If you do not handle the toothache, the toothache makes you feel bad. If you feel bad, you may not do well at work because you are irritable. Not fixing the toothache can lead to further medical complications because it is easy for germs to breed and spread from your mouth. One day you lose your job because you have been missing work due to your chronic illness. Without a job, you cannot pay your rent. If you fail to solve the problem of rent money, you are on the street, homeless, in poor health, eating out of garbage cans, *and* you still have the toothache."

While an extreme example, that story stayed with me. I realized at a young age the importance of solving problems, and the domino effect caused from not solving a problem.

Many people do not solve their financial problems when they are small and at the toothache stage. Instead of solving the problem they make it worse by ignoring it or not solving the root of the problem. For example, when short of money, many people use their credit cards to cover the shortfall. Soon they have credit card bills piling up and creditors hounding them for payment. To solve the problem, they take out a home equity loan to pay off their credit cards. The problem is they keep using the credit cards. Now they have a home equity mortgage to pay off and *more* credit cards.

To solve this credit problem, they get new credit cards to pay off the old credit cards. Feeling depressed because of mounting money problems, they use the new credit cards to take a vacation. Soon they cannot pay their mortgage or their credit cards, and decide to declare bankruptcy. The trouble with declaring bankruptcy is that the root of the problem is still there, just like the toothache. The root of the problem is a lack of financial intelligence, and the problem caused by a lack of financial intelligence is an inability to solve simple financial problems. Rather than address the root of the problem—spending habits, in this case—many ignore the problem. If you don't pull a weed up by the root, and only cut off the top, it will come back quicker and bigger. The same is true for your financial problems.

While these examples may seem extreme, they are not uncommon. The point is that financial problems are a *problem*, but they are a *solution* as well. If people solve problems they get smarter. Their financial IQ goes up. Once smarter, they can now solve bigger problems. If they can solve bigger financial problems they get richer.

I like to use math as an example. Many people hate math. As you know, if you do not do your math homework (practicing solving math problems), you can't solve math problems. If you can't solve math problems, you can't pass the math test. If you can't pass the math test, you get an F for your math course. Getting an F in your math course means you can't graduate from high school. Now the only job you can get is at McDonald's earning minimum wage. This is an example of how one small problem can turn into one big problem.

On the other hand, if you diligently practice solving math problems, you become more and more intelligent, and able to solve more complex equations. After years of hard work, you are a math genius, and things that seemed hard before are now simple. We all have to start at 2 + 2. Those who succeed don't stop there.

The Cause of Poverty

Poverty is simply having more problems than solutions. Poverty is caused by a person's being overwhelmed by problems he or she can't solve. Not all causes of poverty are financial problems. They can be problems like drug addiction, marrying the wrong person, living in a crime-ridden neighborhood, not having job skills, not having transportation to get to work, or not being able to afford health care.

Some of today's financial problems, such as excessive debt and low wages, are caused by circumstances beyond an individual's ability to solve, problems that have more to do with our government and a smoke-and-mirrors economy.

For example, one of the causes of low wages is high-paying manufacturing jobs moving overseas. Today there are plenty of jobs, but they are in the service sector, not manufacturing. When I was a kid, General Motors was the nation's largest employer. Today Wal-Mart is the nation's biggest employer. We all know that Wal-Mart isn't known for its high-paying jobs—or its generous pensions.

Fifty years ago, it was possible for a person without much education to do well financially. Even if you had only a high school degree, a young person could get a relatively high-paying job manufacturing cars or steel. Today, it's manufacturing burgers.

Fifty years ago, the manufacturing companies provided health care and retirement benefits. Today, millions of workers are earning less, while at the same time needing more money to cover their own medical expenses and save enough for retirement. Every day these financial problems are not solved, they grow bigger. And they stem from a larger national problem that is beyond the power of the individual to change or solve. They stem from poor economic policies and cronyism.

The Rules of Money Have Changed

In 1971, President Nixon took us off the gold standard. This was a poor economic policy that changed the rules of money. It is one of the biggest financial changes in the history of the world, yet few people are aware of this change and its effect on the world economy today. One of the reasons so many people are struggling financially today is because of Nixon's actions.

In 1971, the U.S. dollar died because it was no longer money—it became a currency. There is a big difference between money and currency.

The word "currency" comes from the word "current," like an electrical or an ocean current. The word means *movement*. In overly simple terms, a currency needs to keep moving. If it stops moving, it rapidly loses value. If the loss of value is too great, people stop accepting it. If people stop accepting it, the value of the currency plummets to zero. After 1971, the U.S. dollar began moving to zero.

Historically, all currencies eventually go to zero. Throughout history, governments have printed currencies. During the Revolutionary War, the U.S. government printed a currency known as the Continental. It was not long before this currency went to zero.

After World War I, the German government printed a currency in hopes of paying its bills. Inflation exploded and the German middle class had its savings wiped out. In 1933, frustrated and broke, the German people elected Adolf Hitler to power in the hopes he would solve their financial problems.

Also in 1933, Franklin Roosevelt created Social Security to solve the money problems of the American people. Although very popular, Social Security and Medicare are financial disasters about to erupt into massive financial problems. If the U.S. government prints more funny money, i.e. currency, to solve these two massive financial problems, the value of the U.S. dollar will die faster, and the financial problem will get bigger. This is not a future problem. It is happening now. According to a recent report by Bloomberg, the U.S. dollar has lost 13.2 percent of its purchasing power since George W. Bush took office in January 2001.

Nixon's change in the U.S. dollar is one of the reasons so many people are in debt, just as the U.S. government is in debt. When the rules of money changed in 1971, savers became losers, and debtors became winners. A new form of capitalism emerged. Today, when I hear people saying, "You need to save more money," or "Save for retirement," I wonder if the person realizes that the rules of money have changed.

Under the old rules of capitalism, it was financially smart to save *money*. But in the new capitalism, it's financial insanity to save a *currency*. It makes no sense to park your currency. In the new capitalism, currency must keep moving. If a currency stops flowing, it becomes worth less and less. A currency, like an electrical current, must move from asset to asset as quickly as possible. A currency's purpose is to acquire assets, assets that are either appreciating in value or producing cash flow. A currency must move quickly to acquire real assets with real value because the currency itself is rapidly declining in value. Prices of real assets such as gold, oil, silver, housing, and stocks inflate in price because the value of the currency is declining. Their inherent value does not change, only the amount of currency it takes to acquire them.

Gresham's law states, "When bad money comes into circulation, good money goes into hiding." In 1971, the U.S. began flooding the world with funny money—bad money. In the new capitalism, it actually makes more sense to borrow today and pay back with cheaper dollars tomorrow. The U.S. government does it. Why shouldn't we do it? The U.S. government is in debt. Why shouldn't we be in debt? When you cannot change a system, the only way to succeed is to manipulate it.

Because of the 1971 change in money, housing prices have soared as the purchasing power of the dollar has plunged. Stock markets rise because investors are seeking safe havens for their dollars. While economists call this *inflation*, it's really *devaluation*. It makes homeowners feel more secure because their home's value appears to go up. In reality, the purchasing power of the dollar goes down as the net worth of homeowners appears to go up. Higher home prices and lower wages, however, make it harder for young people to buy their first home. If young people do not recognize that the rules of money have changed they will be far worse off than their parents as the U.S. currency continues to devalue.

Another Change in the Rules of Money

Another change in the rules of money occurred in 1974. Prior to 1974, businesses took care of an employee's retirement. They guaranteed the retiree a paycheck for as long as the retiree lived. As you probably already know, that is not the case any longer.

Pension plans that pay an employee for life are called defined benefit, or DB, pension plans. Today, very few companies offer these plans. They are simply too expensive. After 1974, a new type of pension plan emerged, the defined contribution (DC) plan. Today such plans are known as 401(k)s, IRAs, Keoghs, etc. Simply put, a DC plan has no guarantee of a paycheck for life. You only get back what you and your employer contribute . . . if you and your employer contribute anything.

The newspaper *USA Today* found in a survey that the greatest fear in America today is not terrorism, but the fear of running out of money during retirement. One of the reasons for this pervasive fear can be traced back to the 1974 change in the rules of money. And the fear is valid. The U.S. education system doesn't equip its citizens with the financial knowledge required to successfully invest for retirement. If schools teach anything about money, they teach kids to balance their checkbooks, pick a few mutual funds, and pay bills on time— hardly enough financial education to handle the financial problems we face. Beyond that, most people don't realize that the rules of money have changed and that if they are savers, they are losers. Underfunded retirement plans will be the next major U.S. economic crisis.

Government Safety Nets?

This lack of a secure financial future led to Social Security and Medicare, government safety nets created to solve financial problems for people who do not know how to solve their own problems. Both plans are bankrupt. Medicare is already operating in the red. Social Security will soon be operating in the red. In 2008, the first of 78 million baby boomers begin to retire, and most of them do not have enough retirement income to survive on. According to the U.S. government, the obligations for Social Security are approximately $10 trillion, and the obligation for Medicare is $64 trillion. If these numbers are accurate, that means the $74 trillion owed to retirees by the U.S. government is more money than all the money available in all the world's stock markets. This is a big problem that needs financial intelligence to solve. Throwing more money at the problem will only make it worse. It may even collapse the entire system of funny money, sending the dollar closer to zero.

Why the Rich Get Richer

That the rules of money changed, that those changes make you poorer, and that they are out of your control may seem unfair. And it is. The key to becoming rich is to recognize that the system is unfair, learn the rules, and use them to your advantage. This takes financial intelligence, and financial intelligence can only be achieved by solving financial problems.

Rich dad said, "The rich get richer because they learn to solve financial problems. The rich see financial problems as opportunities to learn, to grow, to become smarter, and to become richer. The rich know that the higher their financial IQ, the bigger the problem they can handle, hence the more money they make. Instead of running, avoiding, or pretending money problems do not exist, the rich welcome financial problems because they know that problems are opportunities to become smarter. That is why they get richer."

How the Poor Handle Money Problems

When it came to describing the poor, rich dad said, "The poor see money problems only as problems. Many feel they are *victims of money*. Many feel they are the *only* ones with money problems. They think that if they had more money, their money problems would be over. Little do they know that their attitude towards money problems is the problem. Their attitude creates their money problems. Their inability to solve, or avoidance of them, only prolongs their money problems and makes them bigger. Instead of becoming richer, they become poorer. Instead of increasing their financial IQ, the only thing the poor increase is their financial problems."

How the Middle Class Handle Money Problems

While the poor are the victims of money, the middle class are prisoners of money. In describing the middle class, rich dad said, "The middle class solve their money problems differently. Instead of solving the money problem, they think they can *outsmart their money problems*. The middle class will spend money to go to school, so they can get a secure job. Most are smart enough to earn money and put up a firewall, a buffer zone, between them and their money problems. They buy a house, commute to work, play it safe, climb the corporate ladder, and save for retirement by buying stocks, bonds, and mutual funds. They believe their academic or professional education is enough to insulate them from the cruel, harsh world of money.

"At the age of fifty," said rich dad, "many middle-aged people discover that they are a prisoner in their own office. Many are valued employees. They have experience. They earn enough money, and have enough job security. Yet deep down they know they are trapped financially, and they lack the financial intelligence to escape from their office prison. They look forward to surviving fifteen more years when, at age sixty-five, they can retire and then begin to live, on a leaner budget, of course."

Rich dad said, "The middle class think they outsmart their money problems by being smart academically and professionally. Most lack financial education, which is why most tend to value financial security rather than take on financial challenges. Instead of becoming entrepreneurs, they work for entrepreneurs. Instead of investing, they turn their money over to financial experts to manage their money. Instead of increasing their financial IQ, they stay busy, hiding in their offices."

How the Rich Handle Money Problems

When looking at financial intelligence, it becomes easy to see that there are *five core intelligences* an individual must develop to become rich. This book is about those five financial intelligences.

This book is also about integrity. When most people think of the word "integrity," they think of it as an ethical concept. That is not what I mean when I use the word. Integrity is wholeness. According to *Webster's*, it is "the quality or state of being complete or undivided." A person who has mastered the five financial intelligences I write about in this book has achieved financial integrity.

When the rich have money problems, they use their financial integrity, developed through many years of facing and solving problems with the five financial intelligences, to solve those problems. If the rich don't know the answer to their money problems, they don't walk away and throw in the towel. They seek out experts who can help them solve their problems. In the process, they become financially more intelligent and are that much more equipped to solve the next problem when it comes around. The rich don't quit. They learn. And by learning, they grow richer.

Solving Other People's Financial Problems

Rich dad also said, "Many people work for rich people, solving rich people's money problems." For example, an accountant goes to work to count the rich person's money. The salesperson sells the rich person's products. The office manager manages the rich person's business. The secretary answers the rich person's phones and treats the rich person's customers respectfully. The maintenance man keeps the rich person's buildings and machines running smoothly. A lawyer protects the rich person from other lawyers and lawsuits. A CPA protects the rich person's money from taxes. And the banker keeps the rich person's money safe.

What rich dad was getting at was that most people work at solving other people's money problems. But who solves the worker's money problems? Most people go home and are faced with many problems, money being one of them. If a person fails to handle his or her money problems at home, the problem, like a toothache, leads to other problems.

Many of the poor and middle class work for the rich and then fail to solve their own money problems at home. Instead of looking at financial problems as opportunities to get smarter, they go home, sit in the lawn chair, have a drink, put a steak on the grill, and watch TV. The next morning, they return to work once again solving someone else's problems and making someone else richer.

Poor Dad's Solution

My poor dad tried to solve his money problems by going back to school. He liked school. He did well in school, and felt safe. He obtained higher degrees, and became a PhD. With advanced degrees, he looked for a higher-paying job. He tried to outsmart his money problems by becoming academically and professionally smarter, but failed to become financially smarter. He was a well-educated, hardworking man. Unfortunately, being well-educated and hardworking did not solve his money problems. His money problems only grew bigger as his income went up because he avoided financial problems. He tried to solve his financial problems with academic and professional solutions.

Rich Dad's Solution

My rich dad looked for financial challenges, which is why he started businesses and actively invested. Many people thought he did what he did only to make more money. In reality, he did what he did because he loved financial challenges. He looked for financial problems to solve, not just for the money, but to make him smarter and to increase his financial IQ. Rich dad often used the game of golf as a metaphor to explain his money philosophy. He would say, "Money is my score. My financial statement is my scorecard. Money and my financial statement tell me how smart I am and how well I am playing the game." Simply put, rich dad got richer because the game of money was his game . . . and he wanted to be the best he could be at his game. As he got older, he got better at his game. His financial IQ went up and the money poured in.

Playing the Game

In the following chapters, I will go into the five financial intelligences people need to develop if they want to increase their financial IQ and achieve financial integrity. While developing the five financial intelligences may not be easy and may take a lifetime to develop, the good news is that very few people know of the five financial intelligences, much less have the drive to develop their financial IQ and improve their score. Just by knowing these intelligences you are better equipped than 95 percent of society to solve your money problems.

Personally, my days are dedicated to increasing the five financial intelligences. For me, my financial education never stops. At the start, my process to increase my financial IQ was difficult and clumsy . . . just like my golf game. There was a lot of failure, a lot of money lost, a lot of frustration, and a lot of personal doubt.

At first, my classmates made more money than me. Today, I make much more money than most of my classmates. While I do enjoy the money, I work primarily for the challenge. I love learning. I work because I love the game of money, and I want to be the best I can be at my game. I could have retired a long time ago. I have more than enough money. But what would I do if I retired? Play golf? Golf is not my game. Golf is what I do for fun. Business, investing, and making money is my game. I love my game. I am passionate about the game. So if I retired, I would lose my passion, and what is life without passion?

Who Should Play the Game of Money?

Do I think everyone should play this game of money? *My answer is, like it or not, everyone is already playing the game of money*. Rich or poor, we are all involved in the game of money. The difference is some people play harder, know the rules, and use them to their advantage more than others. Some people are more dedicated, more passionate, more committed to learning and to winning. When it comes to the game of money, most people are playing—if they know they are playing at all—not to lose rather than playing to win.

Since we are all involved in the game of money anyway, better questions may be:

- Are you a student of the game of money?
- Are you dedicated to winning the game?
- Are you passionate about learning?
- Are you willing to be the best you can be?
- Do you want to be as rich as you can be?

If you are, then read on. This book is for you. If you are not, there are easier books to read and easier games to play. For just as in the game of golf, there are many professional golfers but only a few rich professional golfers.

In Summary

In 1971 and 1974, the rules of money changed. These changes have caused massive financial problems worldwide, requiring greater financial intelligence to solve them. Unfortunately, our government and schools have not addressed these changes or the problems. So the financial problems today are monstrous. In my lifetime, America went from the richest country in the world to the biggest debtor nation in the world.

Many people hope the government will solve their financial problems. I do not know how the government can solve your problems when it cannot solve its own money problems. In my opinion, it is up to individuals to solve their own problems. The good news is that if you solve your own problems you get smarter and richer.

The lesson to be remembered from this chapter is that, rich or poor, we all have money problems. The only way to get rich and increase your financial intelligence is to actively solve your money problems.

The poor and middle class tend to avoid or pretend they

do not have money problems. The problem with this attitude is that their money problems persist, and their financial intelligence grows slowly, if at all.

The rich take on financial problems. They know that solving financial problems makes them smarter, and increases their financial IQ. The rich know that it is financial intelligence, not money, that ultimately makes you rich.

The problem with the poor and middle class is they don't have enough money. The rich have the problem of too much money. Both are real and legitimate problems. The question is, which problem do you want? If you want the problem of having too much money, read on.

Chapter 2

The Five Financial IQs

There are five basic financial IQs. They are:

Financial IQ #1: Making more money.
Financial IQ #2: Protecting your money.
Financial IQ #3: Budgeting your money.
Financial IQ #4: Leveraging your money.
Financial IQ #5: Improving your financial information.

Financial Intelligence vs. Financial IQ

Most of us know that a person with a mental IQ of 130 is supposedly smarter than a person with an IQ of 95. The same parallels can be drawn with financial IQ. You can be the equivalent of a genius when it comes to academic intelligence, but the equivalent of a moron when it comes to financial intelligence.

Often I am asked, "What is the difference between financial intelligence and financial IQ?" My reply is, "Financial intelligence is that part of our mental intelligence we use to solve our financial problems. Financial IQ is the measurement of that intelligence. It is how we quantify our financial intelligence. For example, if I earn $100,000 and pay 20 percent in taxes, I have a higher financial IQ than someone who earns $100,000 and pays 50 percent in taxes."

In this example, the person who earns a net $80,000 after taxes has a higher financial IQ than the person who earns a net $50,000 after taxes. Both have financial intelligence. The one who keeps more money has a higher financial IQ.

Measuring Financial Intelligence

Financial IQ #1: Making more money. Most of us have enough financial intelligence to make money. The more money you make, the higher your financial IQ #1. In other words, a person who earns $1 million a year has a measurably higher financial IQ #1 than a person who earns $30,000 a year. And if two people each make $1 million a year and one pays less in taxes than the other, that person has a higher financial IQ because he or she is closer to achieving financial integrity by utilizing financial IQ #2: protecting your money.

We all know that a person may have a high academic IQ and be a genius in the classroom but be unable to make much money in the real world. I would say my poor dad, a great teacher and a hardworking man, had a high academic IQ but a low financial IQ. He did very well in the world of academia but did poorly in the world of business.

Financial IQ #2: Protecting your money. A simple truth is that the world is out to take your money. But not all who take your money are crooks or outlaws. One of the biggest financial predators of our money is taxes. Governments take our money legally.

If a person has a low financial IQ #2, he or she will pay more in taxes. An example of financial IQ #2 is someone who pays 20 percent in taxes versus someone who pays 35 percent in taxes. The person who pays less in taxes has a measurably higher financial IQ.

Financial IQ #3: Budgeting your money. Budgeting your money requires a lot of financial intelligence. Many people budget money like a poor person rather than like a rich person. Many people earn a lot of money but fail to keep much money, simply because they budget poorly. For example, a person who earns and spends $70,000 a year has a lower financial IQ #3 than a person who earns $30,000 and is able to live well on $25,000 and invest $5,000. Being able to live well and still invest no matter how much you make requires a high level of financial intelligence. Having a surplus is something you have to actively budget for. Budgeting for a surplus is something we will look at in detail later on.

Financial IQ #4: Leveraging your money. After a person budgets a surplus, the next financial challenge is to leverage their surplus of money. Most people save their financial surplus in a bank. This was a smart idea before 1971—before the U.S. dollar became a currency. Also, after 1974, workers needed to save for their own retirement. Millions of workers did not know what to invest in, so they invested their financial surplus in a well-diversified portfolio of mutual funds, hoping this would leverage their money.

While savings and a diversified mutual fund portfolio are a form of leverage, there are better ways to leverage your money. If a person is truthful, he or she has to admit it doesn't require much financial intelligence to save money and invest in mutual funds. You can train a monkey to save money and invest in mutual funds. That is why the returns on those investment vehicles are historically low.

Financial IQ #4 is measured in return on investment. For example, a person who earns 50 percent on his or her money has a higher financial IQ #4 than someone who earns 5 percent. And someone who earns 50 percent tax-free on his or her money has a higher financial IQ than a person who earns 5 percent and pays 35 percent in taxes on that 5 percent return.

One more point. Many people think that higher returns on investment require higher degrees of risk. That is not true. Later in this book, I will explain how I achieve exceptional returns, and pay very little, if anything, in taxes, all with very low risk. To me, having a well-diversified mutual fund portfolio and savings in the bank is a lot riskier than what I do. It is all a matter of financial intelligence.

Financial IQ #5: Improving your financial information. There is a bit of wisdom that goes, "You need to learn to walk before you can run." This is true with financial intelligence. Before people can learn how to earn exceptionally high returns on their money (financial IQ #4: leveraging your money), they need to learn to walk; that is, to learn the basics and the fundamentals of financial intelligence.

One of the reasons so many people struggle with financial IQ #4: leveraging your money, is because they are taught to turn their money over to financial "experts," such as their banker and their mutual fund manager. The problem with turning your money over to financial experts is that you fail to learn, fail to increase your financial intelligence, and fail to become your own financial expert. If someone else manages your money and solves your financial problems, you can't increase your financial intelligence. Actually, you are rewarding other people for theirs instead—with your money!

It's easy to increase your financial intelligence if you have a strong foundation of financial information. But if your financial IQ is weak, then new financial information can be confusing and have seemingly little value. Remember my example of math geniuses still needing to start with 2 + 2? One of the benefits of being dedicated to your financial education is that over time you will be better able to grasp more sophisticated financial information just as mathematicians are able to do complex equations after years of practicing math problems. But, again, you need to learn to walk before you can run.

Most of us have been in a class, lecture, or conversation where the information went right over our heads. Or we have been in a class where the information was so complex, attempting to grasp what was being said hurt our heads. This means either the teacher is a lousy teacher, or the student needs a little bit more basic information.

Personally, I do pretty well when it comes to financial information. After years of study, I can sit in a room and understand most financial concepts. Yet when it comes to technology, I am a technosaurus rex. I am a dinosaur. I can barely use a cell phone or turn on a computer. Almost everything to do with technology goes right over my head. When it comes to technology IQ, mine is at the lowest level. The point is that we all have to start somewhere. If I tried to take a class on website design, I would be in serious trouble. You need to learn how to turn the computer on before you can try to design websites! The basic level of information required to succeed in the class would be above my head.

My job in this book is to make financial information as simple as possible. My job is to promote the financial understanding of some very complex financial strategies. In this book, my promise to you is that I write only about things I have done or am currently doing. As you know, there are many teachers and authors who tell you what you should be doing, but don't do what they are advising. Many financial experts and teachers do not really know if what they talk or write about actually works. In other words, many people do not *walk their talk*.

For example, many financial experts advise saving money and investing in a well-diversified portfolio of mutual funds.

The problem with that advice is most advisors don't know if it will work over time. It sounds good. It's simple to do. It doesn't require much financial intelligence to follow this advice. My question is, "Will the advice work?" Will the financial advisor guarantee you that this strategy will make you financially secure? What if the dollar plunges to zero and wipes out your savings? What if the stock market crashes as it did in 1929? Will a well-diversified mutual fund portfolio survive a stock market panic and meltdown? What if inflation goes through the roof because the purchasing power of the dollar plunges and a quart of milk is $100? Could you afford it? What if the U.S. government cannot pay the Social Security and Medicare costs of its elderly?

I cringe whenever I hear a financial expert advising, "Save money and invest in a well-diversified portfolio of mutual funds." I want to ask that expert, "Will you guarantee that this financial strategy will work? Will you guarantee that this financial strategy will keep me and my family financially secure for the rest of our lives?" If the financial advisor is honest, he has to say, "No. I cannot guarantee that what I advise you to do with your money will keep you financially secure."

I too cannot guarantee that what I recommend will keep you and your family financially secure in the future. There are simply too many changes and surprises ahead. The world is changing too rapidly. The rules have changed and are continuing to change. Expanding technology is turning poor nations into financial powers, creating more rich people and more poor people, and greater financial problems and opportunities.

The reason I write, create financial products, and emphasize the importance of the five financial intelligences is because I believe the U.S. and the world are in for an economic upheaval as we have never seen. There have been too many financial problems that have gone unsolved. Instead of using financial intelligence to solve them, we have thrown funny money at them. We have used old ideas to solve modern problems. Using old ideas to solve new problems only creates bigger and newer problems. This is why I believe the five financial intelligences are important. If you develop these five financial intelligences, you will have a better chance of doing well in a rapidly changing world. You will be better able to solve your own problems and increase your financial intelligence.

Practicing What I Preach

I want to assure you that I only write about what I do, or have done. That is why much of this book is written in story form, rather than as financial theory. This does not mean I recommend you do exactly what I do, nor does it mean what I do will work for you. I simply want to share with you my experiences, a journey of solving financial problems that continues today. I share with you what I have learned with the intent that it will assist you in increasing your own financial IQ #5: improving your financial information.

I also know that I do not have all the answers. I do not know if I could survive a massive financial disaster. What I do know is that whatever problems or challenges the future holds, I will look at them as simply opportunities to get smarter and increase my financial IQ. Rather than panic, I believe I can adjust and prosper because of my financial intelligence. I wish the same for you, which is why The Rich Dad Company and its products and programs were created. It's not about having the right financial *answers*; it's about having the right financial *abilities*. As my rich dad said, "*Answers* are about the past, and *abilities* are about the future."

We Have Other IQs

We are all different. We have different interests and dislikes. We have different strengths and weaknesses. We have different gifts and geniuses.

I say this because I do not think financial intelligence is the most important intelligence, or the only intelligence. Financial intelligence is simply an intelligence we all need since we live in a world of money—or to be more exact, currency. As my rich dad said, "Rich or poor, smart or not smart, we all use money."

There are many important types of intelligence, such as medical intelligence. Every time I see my doctor, I am grateful that he dedicated his life to developing his intelligence and his gift. I am also glad that I have enough money and insurance to pay for whatever medical challenges I may face. To this, rich dad said, "Money is not the most important thing in life, but money does affect everything that is important." When you think about it, money affects our standard of living, health, and education. Studies show that poor people have poorer health, poorer education, and a shorter life span.

Before going on with the development of our five financial intelligences, *I want to be clear that I do not think financial intelligence is the most important of all intelligences*. Money is not the most important thing in life. Yet if you stop and think about it, your financial intelligence does affect many things that are important to you and your life.

Other Types of Intelligence

Today, there are a number of different intelligences we need to survive and thrive in society. Three important intelligences are:

1. *Academic intelligence.* Academic intelligence is our ability to read, write, do mathematics, and compute data. This is a very important intelligence. We use this intelligence to solve problems like knowing where and when a hurricane might strike and what kind of damage might be expected.

2. Professional intelligence. This is the intelligence we use to acquire a skill and earn money. For example, a medical doctor will spend years developing this very important intelligence. A doctor's skill will earn them a substantial income and solve many people's problems.

In simple terms, professional intelligence is the intelligence we use to solve people's problems, and people are willing to pay money for those solutions. If my car is broken, I am very happy to pay money to the auto mechanic who fixes my car. I am also very happy to pay my housekeeper money. She solves a very big problem for my wife and me. She is important in our life.

In my businesses I have different people who manage different aspects of my businesses. These individuals tend to have great people skills, as well as great technical skills. These people, and their varied intelligences, are essential to my businesses. An important lesson from rich dad was that different businesses require different technical intelligences. For example, in The Rich Dad Company, I need people with excellent business and people skills. In my real estate businesses, I need people with technical skills, such as licensed plumbing and electrical professionals.

3. Health intelligence. Health and wealth are related. Health care, and consequently health, is rapidly becoming the biggest problem facing our world. Social Security is only a $10 trillion problem. Medicare is a *$64 trillion* problem. As you know, there are many people getting rich by making other people sick. The junk food, soft drink, cigarette, alcohol, and prescription drug industries are a few examples. And the costs of these health problems are passed on to you and me in the form of taxes.

A few months ago, I went to a Boys and Girls Club to assist in their financial education program. It was an eye-opening experience. Talking to the staff dentist, I learned that the main reason inner-city kids miss school is because of toothaches. The cause of the toothaches is sugared drinks and a lack of dentists. This leads to poor health and obesity, which can bring on diabetes. Personally, I think it's tragic that the U.S. spends billions fighting a war, yet does not provide health education and health care for all kids.

My point is we need different types of education and intelligences to do well in this brave new world we live in. While I do not think financial intelligence is the most important intelligence, it does affect everything that *is* important.

Not Everyone Needs Financial Intelligence

If you are fortunate enough to have inherited a fortune, you do not need much financial intelligence—as long as you hire people who do. If your plan is to marry for money, again, you do not need much financial intelligence. Or if you were born talented, and the world showers you with money at an early age, you do not need much financial intelligence—unless you're MC Hammer.

Also, you don't need much financial intelligence if your plan is to work for the government and receive a pension for life, or if you work for an old Industrial Age company like General Motors that still has a defined benefit pension plan that will pay you a paycheck and medical benefits for life.

If you are like most people, you will need some financial intelligence to survive in today's world, even if your plan is to live on Social Security and Medicare. In fact, you may need a lot of financial savvy if your plan is to live on such a small amount of money.

Who Needs the Most Financial IQ?

When we examine the CASHFLOW Quadrant pictured below, it will become easier to understand who needs the most financial IQ.

For those who may not have read my second book in the Rich Dad series, *Rich Dad's CASHFLOW Quadrant*, I will briefly explain. The CASHFLOW Quadrant is about the four different groups of people who make up the world of money.

E stands for employee.
S stands for small business, self-employed, or specialist.
B stands for big business, 500 employees or more.
I stands for investor.

For people whose career path is in the E quadrant, they may not think they need much financial intelligence. The same is true for those in the S quadrant.

My poor dad, as a schoolteacher in the E quadrant for most of his life, did not place much value on financial intelligence. That is until he lost his job and entered the world of business. In less than a year, his savings and retirement were gone. If not for Social Security and Medicare, he would have been in serious financial trouble.

My mom, being a nurse, wanted me to become a doctor. She knew I wanted to be rich, and the richest people she knew were doctors. She wanted me to stake my claim in the S quadrant. Obviously, those were the days before malpractice insurance costs went through the roof. Again, being a nurse, she did not see much need for financial intelligence. Her solution for me was to simply get a high-paying job. As you know, there are many people with high-paying jobs who have no money.

If you want to be an entrepreneur who builds a B quadrant business, or a professional investor in the I quadrant, financial intelligence is everything. For those in the B and I quadrants, financial intelligence is essential because it's the intelligence that gets you paid. In the B and I quadrants, the higher your financial intelligence is, the higher your income will be.

Rich dad said to me, "You can be a successful doctor and be poor. You can also be a successful schoolteacher and be poor. But you cannot be a successful entrepreneur or investor and be poor. Success in the B and I quadrants is measured in money. That is why financial intelligence is so important."

In Summary

After 1971, the dollar turned into a currency. In 1974, businesses stopped paying employees a paycheck for life. As a result of these two major changes, financial intelligence became more important than ever. While financial intelligence is important for everyone, it's even more important for certain people, specifically those who plan on staking their professional claims in the B and I quadrants.

One of the reasons our school systems do not teach students much about money is because most schoolteachers operate from the E quadrant, and thus our schools prepare people for the E and S quadrants. If you plan on operating out of the B and I quadrants, then the five financial intelligences are essential, and you won't learn them in school.

In summary, the five financial IQs are:

1. Financial IQ #1: Making more money.
2. Financial IQ #2: Protecting your money.
3. Financial IQ #3: Budgeting your money.
4. Financial IQ #4: Leveraging your money.
5. Financial IQ #5: Improving your financial information.

Financial intelligence is the intelligence we use to solve our specific financial problems, and financial IQ measures, or quantifies, our results.

And now on to financial IQ #1: making more money.

Chapter 3

Financial IQ #1: Making More Money

After four years at the U.S. Merchant Marine Academy at Kings Point, New York, I graduated in 1969 and got my first job with Standard Oil of California sailing on their oil tankers. I was a third mate sailing between California, Hawaii, Alaska, and Tahiti. It was a great job with a great company. I only worked for seven months and then had five months off, got to see the world, and the pay was pretty good at approximately $47,000 a year—that's the equivalent of $140,000 today.

A salary of $47,000 was considered a lot of money for a kid right out of college in 1969. It still is. Yet when compared to some of my classmates, my pay was low. Some of my classmates were starting their careers at $70,000 to $150,000 a year as third mates. Today that would be the equivalent of $250,000 to $500,000 a year as starting pay. Not bad for twenty-two-year-olds fresh out of school.

The reason my pay was lower was because Standard Oil

was a non-union shipping company. My classmates in the higher pay scales were working for union wages.

After only four months as a third mate, I resigned from my high-paying job with Standard Oil and joined the Marine Corps to fight in the Vietnam War. I felt an obligation to serve my country. At the time, many of my friends were doing everything they could to avoid the draft. Many were going on to graduate school; one ran and hid in Canada. Others were coming up with strange diseases and hoping to be classified 4-F, medically unable to be drafted.

I was draft-exempt because I was in a *Non-Defense Vital Industry* classification. Because oil is essential for war, and I worked for an oil company, the draft board couldn't get its hands on me. I didn't have to avoid the war as my friends were doing. Many friends were surprised when I volunteered to go and fight. I didn't have to; I wanted to.

For me, going to war and fighting was not the hardest part of my decision. I had already been to Vietnam in 1966 as a student studying cargo operations in Cam Ranh Bay. From my naïve vantage point, the war actually seemed kind of exciting. I was not concerned about fighting, killing, and possibly being killed.

The toughest part of my decision was the pay cut I would have to take. Marine Corps second lieutenants were being paid $2,400 a year. At Standard Oil, I was making that in two weeks. On top of that, when you factor in that I was working only seven months a year with five months' vacation, I was giving up a lot. I was earning nearly $7,000 a month for seven months and then taking a five-month vacation without pay and without the fear of being fired for not working. Not a bad deal. There are many people who would take that deal today.

Being a great patriotic company, Standard Oil was very understanding when I informed them that I was leaving to serve my country. They said I could have my job back—if I came back alive. My time in the service would also count towards seniority with the company.

To this day, I recall walking out of their San Francisco office on Market Street with this horrible feeling in my stomach. I kept asking myself, "What are you doing? Are you nuts? You don't have to go. You don't have to fight. You're draft-exempt. After four years of school, you're finally making a lot of money." With the thought of going from earning $4,000 a month to $200 a month rattling in my head, I nearly turned around to ask for my job back.

Taking one last look at the Standard Oil building, I drove to Ghirardelli Square to spend money like a rich man at my favorite bar, the Buena Vista. Realizing that I would now be earning $200 a month as a Marine, I knew this might be my last chance to feel rich and spend rich. I had a lot of cash in my pocket, and I wanted to enjoy it.

The first thing I did was buy the bar a round of drinks. This got the party going. Soon I met a beautiful young woman who was attracted to the cash flowing from my wallet. We left the bar. We wined and dined. We laughed and howled. In my mind, it really was *eat, drink, and be merry, for tomorrow I might die.*

At the end of the evening, the lovely young lady shook my hand, kissed me on the cheek, and sped off in a cab. I wanted more, but she just wanted my money. The next morning, I began my drive from San Francisco to Pensacola, where my flight training was about to begin, and in October of 1969 I reported to flight school. Two weeks later, I nearly died when I saw what a $200-a-month paycheck looked like, after taxes.

Five years later, with one year spent in Vietnam, I was honorably discharged from the Marine Corps. My first and immediate challenge was financial IQ #1: making more money. I was twenty-seven years old and had two great professions to fall back on, one as a ship's officer, the second as a pilot.

For a while, I considered returning to Standard Oil and asking for my job back. I liked Standard Oil, and I liked San Francisco. I also liked the pay. I would have started at about $60,000 a year, since Standard Oil counted my time in the Marine Corps towards seniority.

My second option was to get a job as a pilot with the airlines. Most of my fellow Marine pilots were being offered great jobs with a pretty good starting pay of about $32,000 a year. Although the pay was not as good as Standard Oil, being an airline pilot appealed to me. On top of that, whatever the airlines would pay me had to be better than the $985 a month the Marine Corps was paying me to be a pilot after five years of service.

Instead of returning to Standard Oil or flying for the airlines, however, I took a job with the Xerox Corporation in downtown Honolulu. My starting pay was $720 a month. Once again, I took a pay cut. My friends and family thought the war had made me crazy.

Now, you may ask why I would take a job paying only $720 a month in a very expensive city like Honolulu. The answer is found in the theme of this book: increasing financial IQ. I took the job with Xerox not for the pay, but to increase my financial intelligence—especially financial intelligence #1: making more money. I'd decided that the best way for me to earn money was *as an entrepreneur*, not an airline pilot or ship's officer. I knew that if I were to become an entrepreneur, I needed sales skills. There was only one problem: I was terribly shy and dreaded rejection.

My problems were shyness and a lack of sales skills. Xerox was offering professional sales training. They had the problem of needing salespeople. I was looking to become a salesperson. So it was a great deal. We both solved each other's problems. Soon after I was hired, the company flew me to their corporate training headquarters in Leesburg, Virginia. My sales training officially began.

The four years I spent working for Xerox, from 1974 to 1978, were very hard. For the first two years I was almost fired a number of times because I couldn't sell. Not only was I not selling and in danger of losing my job, but I was also not making any money. But I had a goal to become the top salesman in the Honolulu branch, and I faced my challenges with determination.

After the first two years, the sales training and on the street experience began to pay off, and I finally reached my goal of becoming number one in sales at the Honolulu branch. I had solved the problem of being shy and hating rejection, and had learned to sell. Even better, I was making a lot more money than I would have as a ship's officer or an airline pilot. If I had just settled into a job after the war, I would never have overcome my fear of rejection and my shyness, and I would never have reaped the rewards of facing those challenges and conquering them. I learned a valuable lesson from my experience at Xerox: solving the problem was the path to wealth.

Once I reached my goal and became number one in sales, I resigned to take on my next challenge—building a business. Anyone who has built his or her own business knows the first problem is, once again, financial IQ #1: making more money. Since I now had absolutely no money coming in, I had to solve financial IQ #1 quickly.

Before You Quit Your Job

In my previous book, *Before You Quit Your Job*, I wrote about the process of building my first major business, a business that brought to market the first nylon and Velcro surfer wallets. In that book I wrote about the eight components that make up any business, and about how not having all eight of those business components is the reason why so many businesses fail and remain unprofitable. I believe it's a very important book for anyone who wants to be an entrepreneur and start their own business. It is important to read that book before you quit your job.

In the book, I wrote about how my business went to extreme success in about a year, making me a millionaire, and then failed suddenly. I described the feelings of depression and loss, and a strong desire to run away and hide after the business collapsed. I was deeply in debt and facing the biggest financial problem of my life up to that point.

Rich dad, however, encouraged me to face my problems and rebuild the business instead of run and declare bankruptcy. He reminded me that solving this messy problem would increase my financial intelligence. It was some of the best advice I've ever received. Although painful, the process of facing my problem and rebuilding the business was the best education I could have asked for. It took a number of years to solve the problem and rebuild the business, but the process increased my financial IQs #1 through 5 and made me a financially smarter entrepreneur.

Rebuilding the wreckage of my business *was* my business school. The first thing I had to do was put together the eight parts of my business, the B-I triangle. The second thing I had to do was redefine my business by finding a competitive niche. You see, by 1981, the year I was rebuilding the business, the market was inundated by other wallet makers. Nylon wallets from countries such as Korea, Taiwan, and Indonesia were flooding the world market. Prices for wallets dropped from $10 at retail, the price I had established, to $1 a wallet on the streets of Waikiki and the world. Nylon wallets had become a commodity, and as you know, the market for commodities goes to the lowest-priced producer. In order to compete as a commodity, I needed a market niche. I needed to become a brand. That opportunity came in the form of rock and roll.

As described in *Before You Quit Your Job*, I stumbled into the rock and roll business, and saved my business by licensing the rights to use rock band names on my wallets. Soon I was producing wallets for Van Halen, Judas Priest, Duran Duran, Iron Maiden, Boy George, and others. Because I was a legally licensed product, I got my retail price back up to $10 a wallet. Although I now had to pay a royalty to the bands, being a legally licensed rock and roll product opened doors to retailers across America and throughout the world. My business boomed and money came pouring back in.

As I've said, the way to increase one's financial intelligence is by solving the problem in front of you. By 1981, I had solved the problem of rebuilding my business. Then the next problem appeared: beating my low-priced competitors, and the imitators who took my product and were making money while I was losing money.

This problem came in the form of pirates. The very people who copied my first product, the original nylon wallet, were now copying my competitive niche. They started producing the same licensed products I was producing, selling at lower prices, only not paying a royalty to the bands.

After a few months of fighting the pirates, I realized the only people getting rich were my attorneys who were charging me to fight them in court but not winning. The pirates were smarter and quicker than my attorneys. All my attorneys could tell me was that they needed more money to fight. It didn't take me long to realize I was just paying another group of pirates, and these pirates (my attorneys) were supposed to be on my side. I was learning another valuable lesson in business and money, which will be covered in the next chapter—financial IQ #2: protecting your money.

There is a saying that goes, "If you can't beat them, join

them." Tired of hemorrhaging money in a losing battle, I fired my attorneys and flew to Korea, Taiwan, and Indonesia to join forces with the pirates. Instead of fighting them in court, which was costing me much more money than I was making, I licensed my competitors to produce my wallets for me. My production costs dropped, my legal fees went down, and I had better factories behind me. I could now do what I did best—sell. Business boomed again. Soon our products were in department stores and at rock concerts. In 1982, a new television network hit the airwaves, MTV. Our business went through the roof and, once again, money poured in.

In January of 1984, I sold my share of the rock and roll nylon wallet business to my two partners. Kim and I left Hawaii and moved to California to start our business education company. I had no idea there would be such a difference between selling a product and selling education. Nineteen eighty-five was the worst year of our lives. Our savings ran out, and soon the problem of not enough money was a major one. I'd been broke before, but Kim hadn't. That she stayed with me is a testament to her character—not my good looks. Yet, we worked together and built an international business teaching entrepreneurship and investing with offices in the U.S., Australia, New Zealand, Singapore, and Canada. In 1994, Kim and I sold the business and retired with enough passive income from our real estate investments to support us for the rest of our lives.

But . . . we got bored. After our brief retirement, Kim and I produced our board game *CASHFLOW* in 1996, and *Rich Dad Poor Dad* was released as a self-published book in 1997. In mid-2000, Oprah Winfrey had me on her program for an hour, and the rest is history. Today, The Rich Dad Company is an international business. Much of the success is due to lessons learned from the failures and successes of my previous businesses. If I hadn't learned from solving my problems, I would never have made it this far. If I had thrown in the towel and let circumstances overwhelm me, you wouldn't be reading this book right now.

Every Goal Has a Process

As we all know, every worthwhile goal has a process and takes work. For example, to become a medical doctor there is a rigorous process of education and training. Many people dream of becoming a doctor, but the process gets in their way. In the last few pages you just read about my process, and let me tell you, it was work.

One of the reasons people lack financial IQ #1: making more money, is because *they want the money but not the process.* What many people do not realize is that it's the process that makes them rich, not the money. One of the reasons many lottery winners or kids who inherit family wealth are soon broke is because they received the money, but didn't have to go through the process. Many other people fail to become rich because they value a steady paycheck more than the learning process of becoming financially smarter and richer. They are held back by the fear of being poor. It is this very fear that keeps them from taking the chances and solving the problems required to become rich.

We Are All Different

We are all different, and have different strengths and weaknesses. We all have different processes, different challenges, and different problems. Some people are natural salespeople. I wasn't. My first problem was my inability to overcome my fear of selling and the terror of being rejected. Some people are natural-born entrepreneurs. I wasn't. I had to learn to be an entrepreneur.

I make this point because I'm *not* saying you need to learn to sell, or that you need to learn to be an entrepreneur. That was my process. It may not be yours. The first step to increasing your financial IQ #1: making more money, is to decide what the best way for you to make more money is. If it's to become a medical doctor, get ready for medical school. If it's to become a pro golfer, start putting. In other words, choose your goal, and then choose your process. Always remember that the process is more important than the goal.

Emotional Intelligence

At this point it is important to point out that financial intelligence is also emotional intelligence. Warren Buffett, the world's richest investor, says, "If you cannot control your emotions, you cannot control your money." The same is true for your process. One of the toughest parts of my process was not quitting when I was depressed, not losing my temper when I was frustrated, and to continue to study when I wanted to run.

Another reason many people fail in their process is they cannot live without instant gratification. The main reason I mention the low pay I received at the start of my life was to illustrate the importance of delayed gratification. Many will sacrifice a richer tomorrow for a few bucks today. I did not make much money in my twenties and thirties, but I make millions today.

Controlling the highs and lows of my emotions, and delaying short-term gratification, was essential in developing my financial intelligence. In other words, emotional intelligence is essential to financial intelligence. In fact, I would say that when it comes to money, emotional intelligence is the most important intelligence of all. It is more important than academic or professional intelligence. For example, many people fail to chase after their dreams because of fear. If they start, they quit when they fail, and then they blame others when they should be taking responsibility for their failures.

Quitters Rarely Win

There is a young man who worked for me a few years ago. He was very bright, charming, had his MBA, and earned a lot of money. In his spare time, he and his wife tried many business ventures. They tried real estate, and failed. They bought her a small franchise, and failed. Then they bought a nursing home, and nearly lost everything when patients died unexpectedly. Today, both are back at work with high-paying jobs, but an unsettling feeling of inadequacy.

The reason I mention this young couple is because they failed to learn. They let the learning process beat them. When the going got tough, they quit. While it's commendable that they tried new ventures, they stopped when their problems seemed too big to be solved. They failed to push through their failure and learn from their mistakes. They failed to realize that the process, not the money, made them rich.

One of the toughest lessons I had to learn from my rich dad was to stick with the process until I won. When I ran into trouble at Xerox because I could not sell, I wanted to quit. Because I could not sell, I was not making money. In fact, it was costing me more to live in Honolulu than I was earning. Rich dad said, "You can quit when you win, but never quit because you're losing." Not until 1978, after becoming the number one salesperson for Xerox, did I quit. The process had made me richer, both mentally and financially. By overcoming my problem of not being able to sell, I was able to overcome my problem of not making money.

While working at Xerox I started my nylon wallet business in my spare time. In 1978, I went full-time into my wallet business. The business took off, and then failed. Again, I wanted to quit; and again, rich dad reminded me that the *process* is more important than the *goal*. Many times he reminded me, while I was deeply in debt, without much money, that if and when I solved this problem, I would never need money again.

I would know how to build a business, and I would be a little more financially intelligent. But first I had to solve the problem in front of me.

Too Much Money

At the start of this book, I wrote that there are two kinds of money problems. One problem is not enough money, and the other is too much money. In 1974, as I was leaving the Marine Corps, I had to make up my mind which problem I wanted. If I wanted the problem of not enough money, I would take either the job with Standard Oil or the airlines. If I wanted the problem of too much money, I would take the job with Xerox, even if it paid the least. As you know, I took the problem of too much money.

I wanted an education, not just money. I chose Xerox because I knew I could be a ship's officer, and I knew I could be a pilot. I didn't know if I could be an entrepreneur. I knew I could fail. I also knew I would learn the most if I faced the risk of failing. If I let fear of failure—of being poor—win, I wouldn't ever have gotten off the ground.

One of the reasons people do not increase financial IQ #1 is because they stick with what they know. Instead of taking on a new challenge and learning, they play it safe. Now, this doesn't mean you should do stupid and risky things. There are many things we could do but choose not to. For example, I could have chosen to climb Mount Everest. Or I could have signed up for NASA's astronaut program. Or I could have entered politics and run for public office. My point is that I chose my next challenge carefully, not haphazardly. I asked myself, "What will my life be like if I take on this challenge and succeed?" It's the same question I ask you to ask yourself.

Helen Keller, the subject of the great movie *The Miracle Worker*, once said, "Life is a daring adventure . . . or nothing." I agree. In my opinion, one way to increase your financial intelligence #1 is to look at life as a *learning* adventure. For too many people, life is about playing it safe, doing the right things, and choosing job security over life. Your life does not have to be risky or dangerous. Life is about learning, and learning is about adventure.

That is why I didn't go back to sailing ships or flying planes, even though I loved both professions. It was time for a new adventure. Intelligence is not about memorizing old answers and avoiding mistakes—behavior our school system defines as intelligent. True intelligence is about learning to solve problems in order to qualify to solve bigger problems. True intelligence is about *the joy of learning* rather than the fear of failing.

Making More Money

Putting the financial statement and the CASHFLOW Quadrant diagrams together, you may get a clearer picture about your choices for financial IQ #1: making more money.

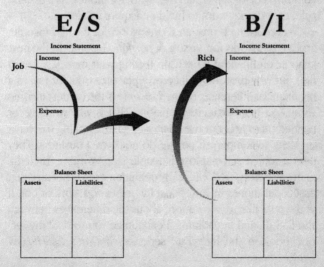

What this diagram explains is that E's and S's work for money. They work for a steady paycheck, for a commission, or by the hour. B's and I's work for assets that produce either cash flow or capital appreciation.

One of the reasons I make more money than my classmates who sailed ships or flew planes is because they worked for paychecks. I on the other hand wanted to build assets as an entrepreneur and acquire assets as an investor. In other words, E's and S's focus on the income column of the financial statement, and B's and I's focus on the asset column.

One of the hardest things to get across to an E or an S is that a B or I doesn't work for money. A B or I technically works for free, which is a tough concept for many to grasp. E's and S's work to be paid, and they must be paid before they work. Working for free, possibly for years, is not in their emotional or professional makeup. E's and S's may volunteer for charities, or work pro bono for worthy causes, but when it comes to personal income, they work for money. As a general rule, they do not work to build or acquire assets.

In accounting terms, an E or S works for *earned* income, and a B or I works for *passive* or *portfolio* income. In the next chapter on financial IQ #2: protecting your money, you will find out why the kind of income a person works for makes a big financial difference. *Earned income* is the hardest income to protect from financial predators. That is why working for *earned income* is not the financially smartest thing to do.

Many self-employed people do not own a business. They own a job. If self-employed people stop working, their income also stops or declines. By definition a job is not an asset. Assets put money in your pocket whether you work or not. If you would like to know more about the differences between the E, S, B, and I quadrants, I encourage you to read my second book in the Rich Dad series, *Rich Dad's CASHFLOW Quadrant*.

Why the Rich Get Richer

Looking at the diagram on this page, it is easy to understand why the rich get richer.

One of the reasons the poor and middle class struggle is that they work for money and a steady paycheck. The problem with working for money is you have to work harder, longer, or charge more to make more money. The problem with physically working harder and longer is that we all have a finite amount of time and energy.

One of the reasons why the rich get richer is that every year they work to build or acquire more assets. Adding more assets does not require working harder or longer. In fact, the higher a person's financial IQ, the less he or she works while acquiring more and better-quality assets. You see, assets work for the rich by producing passive income.

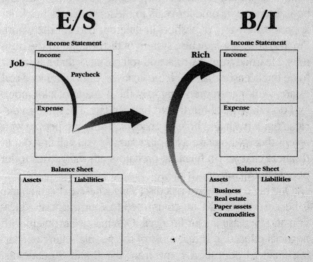

Every year, Kim and I set goals as to how many new assets we want. We do not set goals to make more money. When Kim first started investing in real estate, in 1989, she had a goal of twenty residential properties in ten years. At the time, it seemed like a major task. She started with a two-bedroom, one-bath house in Portland, Oregon. Eighteen months, not ten years, later she blew past her goal of twenty properties. After she reached her goal, she sold the units, taking capital gains of over a million dollars, and upgraded for bigger and better units in Phoenix, Arizona, tax-free.

In 2007, her personal goal is to add an additional 500 rental units to her portfolio. She already has over 1,000 units paying her passive income, the least taxed income, every month. She makes more money than most men, and she has accomplished all of this as an entrepreneur in the I quadrant.

My focus is to increase my cash flow from business assets and commodities. I invest heavily in oil, gold, and silver companies. As an educational entrepreneur, each time I write a book I receive income for years in the form of royalties from approximately fifty publishers in different parts of the world. I'm also adding a franchise system of distribution to the business. I learned from my rock and roll business that it is better to be the licensor than to be the licensee. Although I love real estate, I enjoy entrepreneurship in the B quadrant a lot more.

I do not write about this to brag. In fact, I hesitate to disclose our wealth and how we made it. There are people who resent those who make a lot of money. As you will find out in the next chapter on financial predators, it's dangerous to let people know you are rich.

One big reason why I risk disclosing what we do and make is because Kim and I are committed to your financial education and increasing your financial IQ. A massive problem with financial education is that most of the people selling or sharing financial education come from the E and S quadrants. They are employees or self-employed people. Most are not really rich. Many are journalists who write about money but have little money themselves. Or they are salespeople such as stock and real estate brokers. Many of these financial experts have what other E's and S's have. They have retirement plans filled with stocks, bonds, and mutual funds. Many are counting on the stock market for financial survival and will be wiped out if there is a massive market crash during their retirement. Many will struggle if the U.S. dollar continues to decline in purchasing power and inflation takes off. In short, many financial experts handing out financial advice do not know if their retirement plans will work. If they did, many would have retired.

Kim and I know our retirement plan works. We know because passive income pours in every month from our assets. We are not putting money in savings, bonds, or mutual funds for the future. If we are wiped out, which is always possible, our real asset will be our financial IQ. We can rebuild again because we focused more on learning rather than earning. We learned to manage our own money, rather than turn our money over to an E or S. As rich dad said, "Just because you invest or are self-employed, does not mean you are an investor or a business owner."

In Summary

The secret to making more money is found in the following diagram:

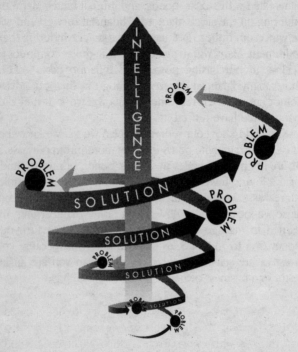

In order to grow wealthy, you must come to terms with the fact that problems will never go away. Each time you find a solution to a problem, a new one will pop up. The key is to realize that the process of solving those problems makes you rich. And once you start solving not only your own problems, but others' as well, then the sky is the limit.

People will pay money for you to solve their problems. For example, I will pay money to my doctor to keep me healthy. I pay money to my housekeeper to keep my house tidy. I shop at my local supermarket because my problem is hunger and starvation if I don't eat. I pay the person who runs a local restaurant for providing great food and a great dining experience. I pay taxes to public servants to provide a well-run government. I put money in the offering plate at church to support my spiritual guidance and education.

Kim makes a lot of money because she solves a big problem, the problem of quality housing at an affordable price. The more she works to solve that problem, the more money she makes. I work hard to solve the problem of the need for financial education.

Simply put, there are trillions of ways to make more money because there are trillions of, if not infinite, problems to solve. The question is, which problems do you want to solve? The more problems you solve, the richer you will become.

Many people want to get paid for doing nothing, and are unwilling to solve any problems. Or they want to be paid more than the problem they are solving is worth. One of the reasons I did not join a union shipping company is because I am a capitalist, not a laborer. In fact, one of the reasons there are fewer U.S. ships today is because it costs too much money to operate a U.S. merchant ship. And that is one reason why most cargo and passenger ships in U.S. ports are not manned with U.S. citizens. The high cost of operating a U.S. ship is why so many graduates of my school, Kings Point, cannot find jobs when they graduate today. This is the problem of wanting to be paid more and doing less.

My poor dad was a union man. In fact, he was the head of the teachers' union of Hawaii. I understand his point of view that teachers had more power as a collective group. Without a union, teachers would be paid even less and have fewer benefits. Without a teachers' union, education would suffer more than it suffers today.

My rich dad was a capitalist. Capitalists believe in producing a better product for a better price. If you cannot deliver a better product at a better price to more people, then the market will punish you. In other words, a capitalist gets paid to solve problems, not create problems—unless you make puzzles.

Many think of capitalists as pigs. And many *are* greedy pigs. Yet there are capitalists who do a lot of good, such as provide health care, food, transportation, energy, and communications to the world. As a capitalist who does my best to make the world a better place, my problem is with people who want to be paid for doing nothing or paid more to do less. In my opinion, a person who wants to be paid more and do less, or nothing, is also a greedy pig.

Those who want to be paid more for doing less will find life harder as the world changes. For example, labor unions that demand higher wages and benefits for less work are the major reason why jobs move overseas. Today in America, a unionized autoworker is paid about $75 an hour, including benefits. In China, the same autoworker is paid about 75 cents an hour. As I write, Chrysler has signed a deal with China's Chery Motors to produce cars there. Price: less than $2,500 a car. That is about the same price as health insurance costs add to every American car.

A true capitalist is simply someone who recognizes a problem and creates a product or service to address that problem. You can charge a higher price if your product or service has a higher perceived value, but there needs to be added value. For example, I charge more money for my books and games because to some people there is more perceived educational value in them. For many other people, my books and games are not worth the price. Many do not value my brand of financial education because my brand of financial education does not solve their financial problem. Many people do not believe the rules of money changed in 1971 and 1974, and want to believe that they can keep working hard, saving money, investing in mutual funds, and expecting more pay for less work. For their sake and their families' financial future, I hope those beliefs and actions solve their financial problems.

For your sake, I hope you do not believe that. I have a hunch that you don't, since you are reading this book and actively increasing your financial intelligence by doing so. Begin now to think about what problems you need to solve, engage those problems head-on, and the money will follow. And once you have that money, you're going to need to use every ounce of your financial intelligence to protect it. That's what the next chapter is all about, financial IQ #2: protecting your money.

Chapter 4

Financial IQ #2: Protecting Your Money

Protecting your money from financial predators is important. As most of us know, the world is filled with people and organizations waiting for the opportunity to help themselves to your money. Many of these people and organizations are very smart and powerful. If they are smarter than you, or have more power than you, they will get your money. This is why financial IQ #2 is so important.

How Do You Measure Financial IQ #2?

Financial IQ #1 is generally measured in gross dollars. Financial IQ #2 is measured in percentages. Here's what I mean. The following are three examples of three different percentages:

1. In America a person who earns $100,000 a year from wages may pay as much as 50 percent in combined

taxes such as federal, state, and FICA. This person's net after-tax income is $50,000.

2. Another person earns $100,000 income from their investments and pays 15 percent in taxes. This person's net after-tax income is $85,000.

3. A third person earns $100,000 income and pays 0 percent in taxes. This person's net after-tax income is $100,000.

In the examples above, the person who pays the least percentage in taxes has the highest financial IQ #2: protecting your money, because less money is lost to financial predators.

In later chapters, I will go into how to earn a lot of money and pay nothing in taxes, legally. But for now, keep this simple idea in mind: financial IQ #2 measures the percentage of income a person keeps against the percentage of income financial predators take.

Bunnies, Birds, and Bugs

Rich dad's lessons to his son and me on the importance of protecting money from financial predators started at a very early age—before we had any money. Because we were young, rich dad used a very simple example of farmers to make his point. He said, "A farmer needs to protect his crops from bunnies, birds, and bugs. Bunnies, birds, and bugs are thieves to a farmer."

Using the idea that bunnies were thieves served as a powerful lesson to me as a young boy. Bunnies were cute and cuddly. They were harmless. The same was true of birds. In fact, I had a pet parakeet at home and to label a bird a thief was a harsh concept. Bugs, however, I understood. I knew how they could be labeled thieves. I had a garden at home, and I lost many of my vegetables to bugs.

Standing behind Us

Rich dad was not trying to frighten us. He simply wanted his son and me to be aware of the real world. The reason he used cute creatures such bunnies and birds was to make the point that some of the biggest thieves of our personal wealth are not just bandits, criminals, or outlaws. He used bunnies and birds because he wanted us to remember that some of the greatest financial predators are people and organizations that we love, trust, or respect—people or organizations we think are on our side and are *standing behind us*. Rich dad said, "The reason so many people stand behind us is because it is easier to get into our pockets from that position. One of the reasons so many people have financial problems is because they have too many hands in their pockets."

Continuing on with his "B" theme of bunnies, birds, and bugs for labeling farmers' predators, rich dad's list of real-world financial predators included: bureaucrats, bankers, brokers, businesses, brides/beaus, brothers-in-law, and barristers.

The First B: Bureaucrats

As we all know, taxes are our single largest expense. The job of the tax department is to get your money and turn it over to a government bureaucrat who spends it.

Unfortunately, the problem with most politicians and bureaucrats is that they are very good at spending money. Most public servants do not know how to make money, which may be why they choose to become bureaucrats. If they could make money they would probably be businesspeople instead of bureaucrats. Since they do not know how to make money, but love to spend it, bureaucrats spend a lot of time figuring out more and creative ways to take our money via taxes.

For example, American bureaucrats created a clever tax program known as the AMT, which stands for *alternative minimum tax*. The AMT was created in 1970. It is an additional tax on high-income workers earning approximately $60,000 or more a year. It's a clever way to tax a person twice on the same income. The problem is, $60,000 was a lot of money in 1970. Today, $60,000 is hardly a high income. Many of the rich do not pay this tax . . . only high-income workers do.

As you know, we already pay taxes on our income, investments, homes, cars, gasoline, travel, clothing, meals, alcohol, cigarettes, businesses, education, permits, licenses, death, and on and on. We pay taxes upon taxes. We pay taxes on taxes we do not even know about. These taxes are sold to us as being good for society, and some are. Society's problems, however, only get bigger because bureaucrats do not know how to solve problems (and consequently do not know how to make money); they only know how to throw money at problems. When more money does not solve a problem they create new taxes with clever names. Since the problems only get bigger, the percentage we pay in taxes only goes up. Just as compounding interest makes us richer, compounding taxes makes us poorer. This is one reason why financial IQ #2 is so important. You cannot become rich if all the money you make is taken from you by financial predators.

TAXES ARE IMPORTANT

Before going on, I need to say that I am not against the government or paying taxes. Rich dad said, "Taxes are an expense for living in a civilized society." He pointed out to his son and me that taxes pay for schools and teachers, fire and police protection, court systems, the military, roads, airports, food safety, and the general operation of the business of government. Rich dad's frustration with taxes was that bureaucrats very rarely solved the problems they faced, which meant taxes had to keep going up. Instead of solving the problem, a bureaucrat often calls for a committee to study the problem, which means nothing will be done. Realizing that we will only pay more in taxes, rich dad's philosophy was, "A bureaucrat's job is to get their hands deeper in your pockets—legally— and your job is to have them take as little as possible— legally."

Unfortunately, it is often the people who earn the least who pay the highest percentage in taxes. At a recent event, Warren Buffett had this to say about the U.S. tax system: "The 400 of us [here] pay a lower part of our income in taxes than our receptionists do, or our cleaning ladies, for that matter. If you're in the luckiest 1 percent of humanity, you owe it to the rest of humanity to think about the other 99 percent."

WHICH POLITICAL PARTY IS BETTER?

Just so you know, I am not Republican or Democrat, conservative or liberal, socialist or capitalist. When asked, I simply reply that I am *all of the above*. For example, as a capitalist, I want to make a lot of money and pay as little in taxes as possible. As a socialist, I make tax-deductible donations to charities and worthy causes, and I want my taxes to provide for a better society and care for those who truly cannot care for themselves.

Many people believe that Republicans are better than Democrats when it comes to money. The facts do not support their belief. Republicans say, "Democrats tax and spend." Republicans, on the other hand, *borrow and spend*. The net result, regardless of party, is increasing long-term national debt, a debt that will be passed on to future generations in the form of higher taxes. This is a sign of low financial IQ.

It was Democratic presidents Roosevelt and Johnson who are credited with creating Social Security and Medicare, two of the most expensive and potentially disastrous programs in world history.

America was the world's biggest *creditor* nation under Republican president Dwight D. Eisenhower. We were a rich nation. When Republican Richard Nixon became president, however, the rules of money changed, and the wealth of the U.S. began to change. As president, Nixon took us off the gold standard in 1971. This converted the dollar from money to a currency.

Nixon allowed the U.S. government to print as much money as necessary to solve our money problems. This is the same as a person writing checks without having any money in the bank. If we did what the government does today, we would be in jail. One of the reasons for the growing gap between the rich and everyone else is that most people are still working by the old rules of money——the old capitalism. After 1971, the new rules of money took over. The rich became richer and the poor and middle class worked harder trying to keep from falling between the cracks.

In 1980, Republican president Reagan gave us *supply-side economics*, a.k.a. "voodoo economics." The new economic theories promoted by the Great Communicator Reagan, an actor not an economist, were the illusion that we could cut taxes and continue to pay the government's bills by borrowing money. This is the same as taking a cut in pay and using credit cards to pay bills.

When Thomas Gale Moore, then a member of President Reagan's Council of Economic Advisors, noticed that the United States was crossing the creditor/debtor threshold in the mid-1980s, he said not to worry: "We can pay off anybody by running a press." Call me crazy, but usually that's called counterfeiting.

Because of the 1971 change in our money, and Reagan's supply-side economics, the national debt of the U.S. exploded. By the end of Reagan's reign, the federal debt was $2.6 trillion.

President Reagan's vice president, the first George Bush,

realizing the national debt was exploding due to the loss of revenue from Reagan's tax cuts, ran for president promising, "Read my lips, no new taxes." After he was elected, he raised taxes and was not reelected.

Then President Clinton, a Democrat, entered office. After having a little trouble with his zipper, he left office claiming to have balanced the budget and not increased the national debt. Of course, just as he lied about his sex life, he lied about balancing the budget. He "balanced" the budget by counting tax dollars for Social Security and Medicare as income. Instead of the money going into the Social Security trust fund, he spent it. That would be like him taking money from his daughter's college fund to buy a new dress for Monica.

Clinton, however, did speak one truth during his term of office. He admitted that there was no such thing as a Social Security trust fund. During his presidency, Medicare began to operate in the red, meaning more money was going out than coming in. Soon, Social Security will be in the same predicament, as 78 million baby boomers begin to retire in 2008.

Enter the second President Bush. Uniting the world after 9/11, he then used his popularity to wage war against Iraq, on unsubstantiated claims. Today, he is one of the most unpopular presidents in history. Not only was the war a disaster, but in order to prevent a disaster in the economy, the Federal Reserve Bank cut interest rates and flooded the world with funny money under his watch. After just five years in office, President Bush has borrowed more money than all other U.S. presidents in history combined. The current subprime crisis is the fruit of his economic policies.

All of this is to say it doesn't matter which party is elected into office. If it's Democrats, they will probably *tax and spend*. If it's Republicans, they will probably *borrow and spend*. The net result is the same: greater debt, bigger financial problems, and higher taxes. All funded by taking as much of *your* money as possible.

ARE YOU A CAPITALIST OR A SOCIALIST?

There is a joke I heard years ago, explaining the difference between a socialist and a capitalist. One day a socialist knocked on a farmer's door and asked him to join the local socialist party. Not knowing what a socialist was, the farmer asked for an example of socialist behavior. The socialist said, "If you have a cow, then everyone in the village can have some of the milk from your cow. It's called sharing the wealth."

"That sounds good," said the farmer.

"And if you have a sheep," the socialist said, "then everyone shares in the wool."

"Very nice," said the farmer. "This socialism sounds good."

"That's great," said the socialist, believing that he had a convert to socialism. "And if you have a chicken, then everyone shares in the eggs."

"What?" the farmer screamed angrily. "That's terrible. Get out of here and take your socialist ideas with you."

"But, but, but," stammered the socialist, "I don't understand. You were happy with the idea of sharing milk and wool. Why do you object to sharing eggs?"

"Because I *don't have* a cow or a sheep," snarled the farmer. "But I do have a chicken."

And this is why financial IQ #2 is so important. Everyone agrees that we need to share the wealth, as long as it is *your* wealth, not *their* wealth.

CHOOSE YOUR INCOME CAREFULLY

From previous chapters, you already know that there are three different types of income: *earned, portfolio,* and *passive.* Knowing the differences is important, especially when it comes to protecting your money from bureaucrats. Working for *earned income* does not allow for much protection from predatory taxes.

In America, even low-income wage earners pay a high percentage in taxes. Workers approximately pay a 15 percent tax for Social Security, and they also pay federal, state, and local taxes. Now, I can hear some people saying that Social Security is not a 15 percent tax. They think it is more like 7.4 percent, and that your employer pays the other 7.4 percent. That may be true, but my way of looking at the combined 15 percent is that it is my money. If my employer did not pay it to the government my employer should pay it to me.

The same is true with employees who think their employer matches their 401(k) retirement money. That money, paid by the employer to an investment banker for safekeeping, is still your money.

Personally, I do not want the government managing my future financial security. The government does a horrible job. I'd rather take care of my own money. The government does not have much financial intelligence. It spends the money it collects. The powers that be know that most people are not financially educated. So why not make themselves and their friends rich with your money?

The Second B: Bankers

Banks were created to protect your money from bandits. But what if you found out your banker were also a bandit? A banker does not have to put his hands in your pocket. You take money out of your pocket with your own hands and turn it over to the banker. But what if you found out that the very people you entrusted with your money were siphoning off more money than you knew about—and doing it legally?

While he was New York attorney general, New York Governor Eliot Spitzer investigated a number of investment banking firms and large mutual fund companies, finding them guilty of several illegal practices. The very people the public entrusted with its money were skimming a little more money than they should have been. The guilty companies were fined a trifling amount compared to the dollar amounts they took. While the paltry size of the fines is disturbing, what is even more disturbing is that these bankers are still in business today.

The problem is that Eliot Spitzer's investigation was limited to investment banking firms in New York City. The problem of bankers' taking money from innocent customers is a worldwide one. As more businesses stop caring for workers for life, more workers are forced to save for their own retirement. Workers do not have the money to hire professional financial services like businesses do. This is causing the pool of financially naïve money to grow like a hot-air balloon, making bankers and people who sell financial services to workers grow richer and richer. Today, workers' retirement funds are fueling a global economic boom. Retirement funds are an ocean of money, unprecedented in world history, guarded by bankers, not you.

THE INVESTIGATION BEGINS

In 2007, the Congress of the United States opened an investigation into the current 401(k) pension plans and mutual funds facilitated by the bankers we trust with our money. The following is an excerpt from an article that appeared in the March 14, 2007, edition of the *Wall Street Journal* (Eleanor Laise, "What Is Your 401[k] Costing You?"):

> 401(k) plans aren't required to make clear how much participants are being charged in fees. And there can be a lot of them, including charges to cover independent audits; tracking and maintaining accounts; advisory services; as well as help lines, and of course the basic expense of managing funds in a plan . . .
>
> The growing tension over 401(k) expenses spurred

federal lawmakers . . . last week to probe whether spotty disclosure of fees make it difficult for employees to know if they are getting a good deal.

The problem with these fees is that even your employer can't understand them. In fact, your employer doesn't even know about some of them because they are hidden. So how can you be expected to know or understand the fees? The article goes on to say:

> Now some employers are hiring outside consultants just to help them understand the fees . . .
>
> One area of concern [is] the high fees, complexity and potential conflicts of interest associated with so-called revenue-sharing agreements. These often involve payments by a mutual-fund company to a 401(k) plan provider to compensate the provider for services such as account maintenance. These costs are often built into the expenses of the funds offered in the plans, and help to increase the cost to plan participants.

In reading the excerpt above, it becomes apparent how easy it is for retirement fund providers, that is, bankers, to grow rich off your money. As I mentioned earlier, banks were created to protect your money. Now they work to take it from you. The tragedy of the situation is that we make it so easy for them. We don't even have to walk into the bank anymore (in fact they might even charge you for that!). Instead, money is taken directly from paychecks before it even reaches our hands. Bankers don't have to take it from our pockets because it never even goes into our pockets.

CLIPPING COINS

During the Roman Empire, many emperors played games with their coins. Some clipped the coins, shaving a little gold and silver from the edges. This is why coins today have grooves on the edge. Grooves were to protect coins from clippers. When they could no longer clip coins, the emperors had their treasuries begin mixing the gold and silver with cheaper base metals.

The U.S. government did the same thing with its coins in the 1960s. Suddenly, silver coins disappeared and fake coins took their place. Then in 1971, the U.S. dollar became funny money because it was taken completely off the gold standard.

In many ways, banks are the biggest financial predators of all. Every day, they rob savers of their wealth by printing more and more funny money. For example, the bankers' rules allow them to take in your savings and pay you a small percentage interest. Then for every dollar you save, the bank is allowed to lend out at least twenty more dollars and charge a higher interest on that money. For example, you deposit one dollar and the bank pays you 5 percent interest for that dollar over a year. Immediately, the bank is allowed to lend out twenty dollars and charge you 20 percent interest to use your credit card. The bank pays you 5 percent for one dollar and makes 20 percent on twenty dollars. That is how bankers get rich. If you and I did this, we would go to jail. It is known as usury.

It also causes inflation. Because our banks are playing games with money, the gap between rich and poor becomes larger. Today savers are losers, and bankers are winners.

In the new rules of money, we need to know how to borrow *currency* to acquire assets, since we no longer save *money*. In other words, smart borrowers are the winners in the new capitalism, not those who save money in a bank savings account.

The Third B: Brokers

"Broker" is another word for "salesperson." In the world of money there are brokers for stocks, bonds, real estate, mortgages, insurance, businesses, etc. One of the problems today is that most people are getting their financial advice from salespeople, not rich people. If you meet a rich broker, you need to ask if the broker got rich from his or her sales ability or financial ability.

Warren Buffett once observed, "Wall Street is the place people drive to in their Rolls-Royce to take advice from people who ride the subway."

Rich dad said, "The reason they are called brokers is because they are broker than you are."

GOOD BROKERS—POOR BROKERS

One of the problems of not having much money is that good brokers, brokers who know what they are doing, often do not have time for you. They are busy working with their higher net worth clients.

When Kim and I had very little money, one of our biggest challenges was finding a broker who was willing to educate us. Since we didn't have much money, most brokers didn't have much time. We also met many brokers who only wanted to sell to us, not teach us. Yet we kept looking. What we were looking for was a young stockbroker who was just building a client base, one who was smart, a student of their profession, and also an investor. Almost by accident, through a friend of a friend, we met Tom. Initially, we gave Tom $25,000. Fifteen years later, our stock portfolio is in the millions of dollars and growing.

After we were married in 1986, Kim and I began investing in real estate. We decided to start with very little money. We met a lot of bad real estate brokers who sold real estate but did not invest in real estate. If they did invest, it was in mutual funds. Finally, we met John. Starting with $5,000, he helped us grow our real estate portfolio to approximately $250,000. While that may not sound like a lot of growth, it was accomplished in just three years, during a very bad real estate market in Portland, Oregon. Today, our real estate holdings are in the tens of millions and growing.

LESSONS LEARNED

As you know, there are good brokers and bad brokers. Simply put, good brokers make you richer, and bad brokers make excuses. The following is an abbreviated list of things that helped us find and keep good brokers.

1. Both Kim and I took classes on investing in stocks and real estate. Having more knowledge allowed us to tell an educated broker from a salesperson.

2. We looked for brokers who were also students of their profession. Both Tom and John invested a lot of time beyond their minimum professional education requirements in their fields. Tom often invites me to look at businesses he is researching. John is a real estate broker who actually invests in real estate. Today, he is a respected teacher on the subject of real estate investing.

3. We want to know if they invest in what they sell. After all, why should you invest in what they're selling if the broker doesn't have the confidence to invest in the same stocks?

4. We wanted a relationship, not a transaction. Many brokers only want to sell. Both Tom and John had time to have dinner with us even when we had very little money. Both are friends.

THE KEY TO SUCCESS

The key to success is education. Kim, John, Tom, and I are students of investing. We are interested in the same subject. We all want to learn more about the subject. We invest in our subject. Tom does not know much about real estate so we do not talk about real estate with him. John has no interest in the stock market so we do not talk about stocks with him.

One of the reasons our wealth grew was that our knowledge grew. Often I would call John and ask him questions like, "Can you explain to me the difference between cap rates and internal rates of return?" He would take the time to educate me, rather than just sell to me. With Tom, I would call and ask him questions such as, "Can you explain to me the difference between long bonds and short bonds?" Tom was more than happy to play teacher.

One of the reasons The Rich Dad Company has multiday seminars on stocks and real estate is because financial education is important. The teachers who teach our courses are investors who practice what they teach. The Rich Dad Company values financial education because it was the glue for Kim and me to have a strong relationship with our brokers, Tom and John. It was the personal commitment to long-term financial education that allowed all four of us to grow very rich together.

Today, I have stock and real estate brokers calling constantly. All of them claim to have a hot deal that will make me rich. In most cases, all they are interested in is a commission so they can put food on *their* table . . . not *my* table. Good brokers want to put food on both tables.

Again, financial IQ #2 is measured in percentages. Brokers often earn their income in percentages. For example, if I buy a $1 million property, brokers may earn 6 percent of the sale, or $60,000. If that property makes me 10 percent cash on cash return every year, then the broker's fee has been well earned, since I only pay that commission once.

Conversely, if I buy and sell (flip a property or day trade a stock) I pay a commission going in and coming out. This is often called a "round trip" or "slippage." In real estate, a round trip for a flipper may eat 12 percent of the profits, as well as trigger higher taxes. That is not financially intelligent.

TRADERS VS. INVESTORS

People who go "in and out" are traders, not investors. Not only do traders pay higher commissions to brokers, the trader pays a higher percentage in taxes, a.k.a. *short-term capital gains*, for buying and selling. This means the tax department bureaucrats do not consider people who buy and sell for capital gains investors. They consider them professional traders and may even add a self-employment tax onto their earnings. Brokers and bureaucrats win, and traders lose in these types of transactions. Financially intelligent investors know how to minimize predatory transaction fees and taxes by investing wisely and utilizing good brokers.

CHURNING

Years ago, a friend's mother had her account "churned" by her friendly stockbroker. Churning is when the broker is busy buying and selling stocks for the client. In the end, the broker gets the client's money via commissions, and the client's portfolio is drained.

So, before you turn your money over to a broker, choose your broker carefully. At a minimum, ask the broker if you can call some of their clients and talk to them. Remember, good brokers like Tom and John can make you rich, and bad brokers can make you poor.

The Fourth B: Businesses

All businesses have something to sell. If they do not sell, they are out of business. I often ask, "Is this business's product or service making me richer or poorer?" In many cases, the product or service does not make you richer; it only makes the business richer.

Many businesses do their best to make you poorer. For example, many big department stores have their own credit cards—the worst credit cards a person can own. The reason they want you to carry their credit card is because their company gets a kickback from the bank. The business that issues the card is a broker for the bank. Notice that the pattern *broker* and *banker* reappears again.

USING CREDIT CARDS TO BUY POOR PRODUCTS

One of the reasons so many struggle financially is they buy products that make them poorer and then make themselves even poorer by paying for that product for years with high-interest credit cards. For example, if I buy a pair of shoes with a credit card and take years to pay off the credit card bill, I remain poorer for years to come by continuing to pay for a product that made me poorer, not richer. Poor people buy products that keep them poor and take years to pay for those products, while incurring high interest charges.

If you want to be rich, become a customer of businesses that are dedicated to making you richer. For example, I am a long-term customer of a number of investment newsletters and financial magazines. I am also a customer of businesses that sell educational products and seminars. In other words, I am a good customer to some of my competitors. I like spending money on products or services that make me richer.

The Fifth B: Brides and Beaus

We all know that some people marry for money. Both men and women marry for money rather than love. Like it or not, money plays an important role in any marriage. There is a line from the movie *The Great Gatsby* that goes, "Rich girls do not marry poor boys." The line may be a good line in the movie, but the reality is there are poor girls and boys who do marry rich people for their money.

LOVE PREDATORS

Rich dad called people who marry for money love predators. The more money you have, the more they love you. In his much-publicized pending divorce, Paul McCartney may have to give up 50 percent of his estimated $1 billion dollar estate. That is a lot of money. This shows that McCartney has earned a lot of money as a musical genius, but his lack of financial IQ #2 is costing him a lot of money that a little premarital planning might have saved him. My friend Donald Trump says, "Get a prenuptial agreement before you get married." A prenuptial agreement is a sign of higher financial IQ #2. Losing 50 percent of a life's fortune for a few years of marriage is a sign of lower financial IQ #2.

Rich dad used to say, "When you combine love and money, financial insanity, not financial intelligence, often reigns." When Kim and I got married, neither of us had any money, so I know we did not marry for money. Even though we didn't have money, we had an exit strategy planned in case things did not go as we wanted. That is why Kim has her own legal corporations, and so do I. She has her investments, and so do I. If we should split, we don't have to split our assets. They are already split. I am glad to say that we have been happily married since 1986, and the marriage gets better and better, and richer and richer, every year.

EXIT BEFORE YOU ENTER

It's *insane* to think that life is about living happily ever after. Happily ever after is true only in fairy tales. Things change. That is why exit strategies are important for anything of worth. I know it may be uncomfortable to ask for a prenuptial agreement before you marry the man or woman of your dreams. But it's the financially intelligent thing to do, especially in this day and age of a 50 percent divorce rate. When forming a new business with a new business partner, I know it may be difficult to think about a buy-sell agreement or a business dissolution agreement when you are just starting out, but it is financially intelligent to think of your exit before you enter into the agreement.

The next exit strategy is one many people do not like to think about, but it is financially intelligent to think about it before you make the final exit.

The Sixth B: Brothers-in-Law

Death is the final exit. It is another time when predators appear—or I should say vultures. If you are rich, not having a financial IQ can be expensive for your loved ones. Family, friends, and the government show up for your funeral if you are rich. Your brother-in-law's children's grandchildren, children you've never met, suddenly become family and come to cry at your funeral. If you have a high financial IQ, the percentage of your money these grieving relatives receive will be controlled by you, even after you have moved on. Those with a high financial IQ have wills, trusts, and other legal means of protecting their wealth and final wishes from death predators. Just look at Leona Helmsley. She was able to leave $12 million to her dog while stiffing her grandchildren. While that's not what I would suggest, it is proof positive that a high financial IQ will allow you to determine where your money goes, even from the grave.

Before you pass on, plan your exit with an estate planning specialist. If you are rich or plan on being rich, planning your final exit is the financially intelligent thing to do. Do it before you die—only leave the dog out of it.

The Seventh B: Barristers

You may remember the person who sued McDonald's claiming the coffee was too hot. That is an example of a financial predator using the court system to get your money. Millions of people are waiting for any excuse to use a lawsuit to get rich. This is why the seventh B is for barristers, or lawyers. There are lawyers whose sole purpose in life is to take you to court and take your money.

Knowing these predators are lurking, there are three things a financially intelligent person must do:

1. Keep nothing of value in your name. It was my poor dad who proudly said, "My house is in my name." Financially smart people would not have their houses in their names.
2. Buy personal liability insurance immediately. Remember, you cannot buy insurance when you need it. You must buy it *before* you need it.
3. Hold assets of value in legal entities. In the U.S., the good legal entities are C-corporations, S-corporations, limited liability corporations (LLCs), and limited liability partnerships (LLPs). There are also bad legal entities. These are sole proprietorships and general partnerships. Ironically, most small business owners are in bad entities.

The Rules Have Changed

Today, I continue to hear people say, "Work hard, save money, get out of debt, invest for the long term in a well-diversified portfolio of mutual funds." This is old advice, and it's bad advice from the financially ignorant. It's playing the game of money by the old rules.

In America today, workers who work hard to earn more money just pay more and more in taxes. They save money and lose because the dollar is no longer money, but rather a currency that is constantly declining in value. Instead of learning to use debt as leverage to become richer, they work hard to get out of debt. Millions of American workers put money away in a 401(k) retirement plan filled with mutual funds. Due to a lack of financial education in school, workers' wallets are picked clean by schools of financial piranhas.

A Look at History

When you look back at history, it is easy to see the rules of money changing in the U.S. and the world. You already know why saving money is for the financially naïve. This change took place in 1971.

In 1943, the U.S. government, desperate for money to fight World War II, passed a law that allowed the government to take money out of workers' paychecks, before the worker got paid. In other words, the government got paid before the worker got paid. Today in America, if you have a job, you have no protection against taxes. You do not need a CPA because a CPA can do little to protect your money. But if you own a business or are an investor, there are many loopholes in the government net you can swim through. I will go into some of those loopholes in a later chapter.

As you know, in 1974, workers needed to become investors, saving for their retirement. This gave rise to the 401(k). The problem with a 401(k) is that the government plugged this loophole for workers too. Let me explain.

When a person works for money, his or her income is taxed as *earned income*, the most highly taxed income. When a worker withdraws money from his or her 401(k) plan, that income comes out as, you guessed it, *earned income*. Guess what interest from savings is taxed at? Once again: earned income.

This means a person who works hard, saves money, gets out of debt, and saves for retirement in a 401(k) plan is working for the most highly taxed income—earned income. This is not financially intelligent. People following these rules are having their pockets picked clean by predators standing behind them, and demonstrate a low financial intelligence because they give away a large percentage of their income.

A financially intelligent person does not want a big paycheck. A financially educated person would rather be paid royalties or dividends because taxes are lower on these types of income. A knowledgeable investor at least knows enough to invest for *portfolio* or *passive* income.

It is important to note that tax laws are different for different people. Make sure to seek the advice of qualified tax attorneys and tax accountants before making financial decisions.

In 1913, the Federal Reserve Bank of the United States was formed. This date is possibly the most important date in U.S. history, when the rules of global money really began to change. This is the date people who work for a paycheck should remember as the beginning of the attack on their personal wealth.

First of all, the Federal Reserve Bank of the United States is not a government entity. That's a myth. Neither is it a U.S. entity. It is a bank owned by some of the richest people in the world.

When the Federal Reserve Bank was formed, the richest people in the world took control of the monetary system of the richest country in the world . . . and then changed the rules of money.

Today, I hear Americans demanding that the government protect American jobs and American interests. Occasionally, I hear people say, "Buy American," or "Support American businesses." Well, it's too late for that. Those are feeble cries from a desperate people. In 1913, the richest people in the world took control of the world's money supply by taking control of the world's richest economy, the U.S. economy. They changed the rules, and did not tell anyone.

Today, the U.S. is technically a bankrupt economy, a treasury stuffed full with its own IOUs, known as bonds or T-bills, bills that the children of future generations will have to pay. This stealing of wealth goes on as billions of people go to work in the businesses of the rich, save money in the banks of the rich, and invest in the assets of the rich (i.e., stocks, bonds, and mutual funds) via the investment bankers to the rich. The system is intentionally designed to take and control as much of *your* money as possible—legally.

Years ago, in the early 1980s, I read a great book entitled *Grunch of Giants*. The word "GRUNCH" is an acronym for *Gr*oss *Un*iversal *C*ash *H*eist. The book was written by Dr. R. Buckminster Fuller, considered one of the greatest geniuses of our time. I had the good fortune to personally study with Dr. Fuller three times, just before he died in 1983. He has had a tremendous impact upon my life, as he has on many other people who have read his works or studied with him. Harvard University considers him one of their most significant alumni, and the American Institute of Architects recognizes him as one of the greatest designers of our time.

If you can find Dr. Fuller's book, *Grunch of Giants*, I believe it will make a little clearer how the game of money was stolen from the people, and shielded from discovery by our educational system. I believe you will find the book disturbing, especially when you look at what is going on with oil, war, banks, the economy, and education today.

In the book, Dr. Fuller states that the government puts their hands in your pockets via taxation and turns that money over to their friends who control multinational corporations. In other words, our elected officials, congressmen and senators, do not represent the people, they represent big business. Surprise!

In 2003, President George W. Bush and the Republicans in Congress literally forced through the Prescription Drug Benefit bill. This bill is one of the most expensive bills put through Congress in the last twenty years. The cost to the American taxpayer is well over $500 billion. Soon after the bill was passed a number of congressmen and staff were hired by the drug companies, some at multimillion-dollar salaries. This is an example of GRUNCH in action.

Other books you may want to read on this subject are:

The Dollar Crisis by Richard Duncan
The Battle for the Soul of Capitalism by John Bogle
Empire of Debt by Bill Bonner and Addison Wiggin

I believe the value of looking at these four books is that each author comes from a different discipline, and a different point of view. It is not a single group of lunatic-fringe discontents criticizing the system. For example, Dr. Fuller was a futurist. Richard Duncan is an international banker. John Bogle is the founder of the Vanguard Group. Bill Bonner and Addison Wiggin are international investment advisors. Four different books from four different disciplines, all basically saying the same thing: people are playing games with money and stealing it legally.

A New Set of Rules

Personally, I am not trying to change the system. My personal philosophy is that it is easier to change myself than to change the system. In other words, I am not a person who battles the winds that drive windmills. Hence, I am not politically inclined. I don't believe politics or politicians are effective against those who run the world of money. It seems that most politicians, in order to be elected, need to be pawns of the very people who control the world's money. Most financial advisors are employees of these world bankers.

I simply want to know the rules and play by the rules. This does not mean I believe the rules are fair or equitable. They aren't. The rules of money are what they are, and they change regularly. Besides, this new world of money, even though un-fair, has done a lot of good. It has brought tremendous wealth and new products to the world, raising the standards of living everywhere. Quality of life for billions of people is improving. Money has done a lot of good.

Unfortunately, these changes have come at great expense to many countries, our environment, and many people. Many have become very rich taking advantage of the financially naïve. Many have become rich by taking the wealth of others. This is why financial IQ #2: protecting your money, is a very important financial intelligence. Ignorance is bliss, and that's what the financial predators are banking on—your ignorance making them blissfully rich.

Chapter 5

Financial IQ #3: Budgeting Your Money

My poor dad often advised, "Live below your means."

My rich dad said, "If you're going to be rich, you need to *expand* your means."

In this chapter, you will find out why living below your means is not a financially intelligent way to become rich. You will learn about budgeting and that there are two kinds of budgets. One is a *budget deficit*, and the other is a *budget surplus*. The reason financial IQ #3 is so important is because learning how to budget for a surplus is the key to becoming rich and staying rich.

A Budget Is a Plan

One of the definitions of the word "budget" is: *a plan for the coordination of resources and expenditures.*

Rich dad said a budget is a plan. He went on to say, "Most people use their budget as a plan to become poor or middle class rather than a plan to become rich. Most people operate their lives on a budget deficit rather than a budget surplus. Instead of working to create a budget surplus, many people work to live below their means, which often means creating a budget deficit."

The First Type of Budget: A Budget Deficit

The definition of a budget deficit in *Barron's Finance and Investment Handbook* is: "Excess of spending over income, for a government, corporation, or individual." Notice the words "excess of spending over income." Spending more than you make is the cause of a budget deficit. The reason so many people operate on a budget deficit is because it's so much easier to spend money than to make money. When faced with a crippling budget deficit, most people choose to cut back on their spending. Instead of cutting back on spending, rich dad recommended increasing income. He thought it smarter to expand your means by increasing income.

BUDGET DEFICIT OF A GOVERNMENT

When talking about the budget deficit of a *government,* Barron's states, "A budget deficit accumulated by the federal government of the United States must be financed by the issuance of Treasury bonds." In the previous chapters of this book, I wrote about how the U.S. government was financing its problems by selling debt (i.e., treasury bonds) that future taxpayers must pay for. The Social Security trust fund, which does not really exist, is filled with treasury bonds. In other words, because the U.S. government operates a budget deficit, the money that workers and businesses have been paying into the Social Security fund has been used to pay other bills, not to increase the Social Security trust fund. See the top diagram on page 83.

Income Statement

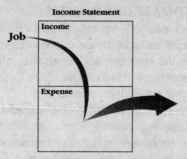

Balance Sheet

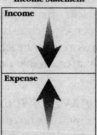

Income Statement

Balance Sheet

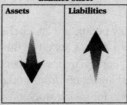

BUDGET DEFICIT OF A BUSINESS

Barron's states, "Corporate budget deficits must be reduced or eliminated by increasing sales and reducing expenditures, or the company will not survive in the long run." Again notice the two choices. One choice is to increase sales and the other is to reduce expenditures.

The financial statement of a corporate deficit looks like the bottom diagram on page 83.

One of the reasons rich dad recommended I take a job with Xerox was that I'd learn to increase sales, which increases income. For many businesses and individuals, increasing income is hard. For businesses that cannot sell, it is easier to cut expenses, increase debt (liabilities), or sell assets. The problem with cutting expenses, increasing debt, and selling assets is that it usually makes the situation worse. Again, this is why rich dad recommended learning to sell. If a person can sell, he or she can increase income. In rich dad's mind, increasing income, rather than reducing expenses, was a better way to solve the problem of a budget deficit. Obviously, if there are frivolous expenses, such as lavish parties, and nonproductive debt, such as a corporate jet, it may be best to address those financially irresponsible problems before trying to sell more.

BUDGET DEFICIT OF AN INDIVIDUAL

Barron's states, "Individuals who consistently spend more than they earn will accumulate huge debts, which may ultimately force them to declare bankruptcy if the debt cannot be serviced."

As we know, many people are in debt because they spend more than they earn. Yet, as stated in the previous chapter, one of the reasons people have less to spend is because financial predators are taking money from workers before they get paid. The justification for taking workers' money *before* they get paid is that most lack the financial intelligence to manage their own money. If our schools had financial education, maybe the workers could be trusted to manage their own money, rather than let bureaucrats and bankers manage their money for them. The problem with letting bureaucrats and bankers manage your money is they think *your* money is *their* money.

Looking at an individual's financial statement, the diagram looks like the one on page 86.

People in the E quadrant often have no control over these four important expenses—taxes, Social Security, pensions, and mortgage payments. From this diagram, you can see how government bureaucrats take money via taxes and Social Security while bankers take your money via pension (401[k]) and mortgage payments. This action is the cause of budget deficits for many people.

A financially intelligent person has control over these expenses.

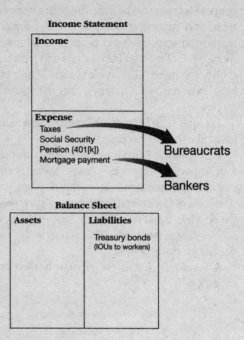

The Second Type of Budget: A Budget Surplus

Barron's states, "A budget surplus is an excess of income over spending for a government, corporation, or individual over a particular period of time."

Notice the words "excess of *income* over spending." This does not necessarily mean living below one's means. The definition does not say a surplus is created due to a reduction of spending, although a reduction of spending may lead to an excess of income. It does mean focusing on creating excess income—financial IQ #1: making more money. Rich dad loved the words "excess of income." This chapter is about excess of income, rather than reducing expenses and living below your means.

BUDGET SURPLUS OF A GOVERNMENT

Barron's states, "A government with a surplus may choose to start new government programs or cut taxes."

There are some issues with this statement. Problem number one is that when governments create a surplus, they spend the money. Here is how government contracts work: if a government agency is efficient and saves money, the agency is punished, instead of rewarded, by having next year's budget reduced. To avoid this, most government agencies spend all their budgeted money, even if they do not need to. This means costs keep going up and the chances of a government budget surplus are slim to none. In other words, government bureaucracies are designed to operate on a budget deficit, and regardless of who is in power, taxes will go up.

How Democrats manage a budget. You may recall from the previous chapter that Democrats love to *tax and spend*. Democrats love to spend on more government social programs like Social Security and Medicare. The problem is, social programs only grow bigger because they fail to solve the problem they are created to address. In order to counteract this, the budget is increased, and the vicious cycle continues. In government, mediocrity is rewarded and efficiency is punished.

The following is a diagram of a Democrat's budget:

Income Statement

Income
Increase taxes

Expense
Increase expenses

Balance Sheet

Assets	Liabilities
Reduce assets	Increase liability via social programs

How Republicans manage a budget. The Republicans tend to *borrow and spend.* They want to expand the economy by flooding the money supply with funny money via debt. It's almost like flooding the economy with legal counterfeit money. Again, extra money looks like an increase in income, but in reality it is an increase in debt in the form of T-bills and bonds, which ultimately diminishes the prospect of a surplus. Many in the middle class do the same thing by using their home as an ATM. Every time their home increases in value, primarily due to the dollar's losing value, they borrow from their home to pay off credit card bills.

Simply said, it's impossible to earn less, borrow and spend more, and create a surplus. As President Clinton so eloquently put it, "It's the economy, stupid."

The following is a diagram of a Republican budget:

Income Statement

Income
Cut budget by reducing taxes
Increase income from debt

Expense
Spend tax dollars on friends' businesses (pork)

Balance Sheet

Assets	Liabilities
	Debt T-bills and bonds

BUDGET SURPLUS OF A BUSINESS

Barron's states, "A corporation with a surplus may expand the business through investment or acquisition, or may choose to buy back its own stock."

Notice the two ways to expand a business: investment or acquisition. A corporation spends to expand, or it buys another company to expand. If a business cannot expand via investment or acquisition, it may buy back its own stock. This stock repurchase may sometimes mean the company feels it is not able to expand the business and opts to buy itself instead. If this action sends its stock price higher, many shareholders will be happy, even though the company is not growing.

Whenever I hear of a company buying back its own stock, I realize it may mean different things. A stock repurchase may mean the company has stopped growing and the leadership does not know how to grow the business. This is not a good sign for investors. Instead of buying more shares as the stock price goes up, it might be time to sell.

A stock repurchase could also mean the leadership thinks its stock price is a bargain compared to the asset value of the company. If this is the case, then investors should be buying more as the stock price rises.

In other words, a budget surplus of a business can tell you different things about the business and its leadership.

BUDGET SURPLUS OF AN INDIVIDUAL

Barron's states, "An individual with a budget surplus may choose to pay down *debt* or increase *spending* or *investment*."

Notice, *Barron's* offers three choices to individuals. These are: paying down debt, spending more money, or investing. As most of us know, one of the reasons so many people have trouble financially is because they increase spending and debt, and reduce investment.

Two Choices

When it comes to financial IQ #3: budgeting your money, there are only two choices—deficit or surplus. Many people choose a budget deficit. If you want to be rich, choose a budget surplus, and create one by increasing income, not reducing expenses.

A BUDGET DEFICIT

I have a friend in Atlanta who makes a lot of money. He has to make a lot of money. If he stops making a lot of money, his money problems will eat him alive. He has chosen to create a budget deficit.

Every time Dan makes more money, he either buys a bigger house, a newer car, or takes an expensive vacation with the kids. He has another bad habit. Every ten years or so, he marries a younger woman and has a new child. Dan grows older, but his wives are always about the same age—twenty-five. Dan is an expert at taking a lot of money and making his money problems worse through deficits.

A BUDGET SURPLUS

The second financial choice is to plan for a budget surplus. After making money, financial IQ #1, and protecting your money, financial IQ #2, learning how to budget for a surplus is essential for achieving financial integrity.

The following are a number of lessons I have learned from my rich dad and other wealthy people about budgeting for a budget surplus.

Budget tip #1: A budget surplus is an expense. This is one of the best financial lessons my rich dad passed on to his son and me. Pointing to the financial statement, he said, "You have to make a surplus an expense." In order to create a budget surplus, his financial statement looked like this:

Income Statement

Income
Expense
Saving
Tithing
Investing

Balance Sheet

Assets	Liabilities

Explaining further, he said, "The reason so many governments, businesses, and individuals fail to create a budget surplus is because they think a budget surplus looks like this:"

Income Statement

Income
Expense

Balance Sheet

Assets	Liabilities
Saving	
Tithing	
Investing	

In *Rich Dad Poor Dad*, I wrote about the importance of *paying yourself first*. Budget #1 is an example of paying yourself first. Budget #2 is an example of paying yourself last.

Most people know they should save, tithe, and invest. The problem is, after paying their expenses, most people don't have any money left to do so. The reason is because they consider saving, tithing, and investing as a last priority.

Let me illustrate what I am saying. Again, looking at the financial statement you can tell a person's priorities.

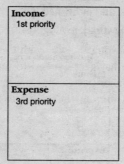

In other words, most of the middle class's financial priorities are:

Priority #1: Get a high-paying job.
Priority #2: Make the mortgage and car payments.
Priority #3: Pay bills on time.
Priority #4: Save, tithe, and invest.

In other words, paying themselves first is their last priority.

A Surplus Must Be a Priority

In order to create a budget surplus, a surplus must be a priority. The best way to make a surplus a priority is to repri-oritize your spending habits. Make saving, tithing, and investing at least priority #2, and list them as an expense on your financial statement.

EASIER SAID THAN DONE

I know most of you can agree with the logic of what I am saying and agree that people need to make saving, tithing, and investing a higher priority. I also know this is easier said than done. So let me tell you how Kim and I handled this problem.

Soon after we were married, we had the same financial problems many newlyweds have. We had more expenses than income. To solve this problem, we hired Betty the Bookkeeper. Betty was instructed to take 30 percent of all income off the top, as an expense, and put that money in the asset column.

Using simple numbers as an example, if we had $1,000 in income, and $1,500 in expenses, Betty was to take 30 percent of the $1,000, and put that money in the asset column. With the remaining $700, she was to pay the $1,500 in expenses.

Betty nearly died. She thought we were nuts. She said, "You can't do that. You have bills to pay." She almost quit. You see, Betty was a great bookkeeper, but she budgeted like a poor person. She paid everyone else first and herself last. Since there was rarely anything left over, she paid herself nothing. Her creditors, the government, and bankers were all more important than Betty.

Betty argued and fought. All of her training told her to pay everyone else first. The thought of not paying her bills or taxes made her weak in the knees.

I finally got her to understand she was doing us a favor. She was helping us out. I explained to her that she was helping us solve a very big problem, the problem of not having enough money, and as you know, solving problems makes us smarter. When she understood she was actually creating income through expense, she was willing to go along with our plan to create a budget surplus. For every dollar of income, Betty would take 30 cents and put it in savings, tithing, and investing. She knew that saving, tithing, and investing were a necessary expense to create a surplus, our first and most important expense.

With the 70 cents from every dollar left, she was to pay taxes, liabilities such as our mortgage and car payments, and then our bills such as electricity, water, food, clothing, etc.

Needless to say, for a long time we came up short every month. Although we had paid ourselves first, we did not have enough money to pay others. There were some months Kim and I came up as much as $4,000 short. We could have paid the $4,000 from our assets, but that was our money. The asset column belonged to us.

Instead of panic, Betty was instructed to sit down with us and let us know how short we were each month. After taking a deep breath, Kim and I would then say, "It's time to get back to financial IQ #1: making more money." With that, Kim and I would hustle around doing whatever we could to make more money. Kim, with her marketing background, often called businesses and offered to consult with them on their marketing plans. She also took modeling jobs and sold a line of clothes. I offered to teach investment or sales and marketing classes. For a few months, I trained sales teams at a local real estate company. I even made money by helping a family move, and by clearing some land for another family.

In other words, we swallowed our pride and did whatever it took to make the extra money. Somehow, we always made it; and somehow Betty stuck with us and assisted us with our problem, solution, and process, even though she worried more about us than we did.

Unfortunately, Betty could help us but was unwilling to help herself. Last we heard, she retired and moved in with her single daughter. They share expenses, using Betty's payments from Social Security to pay them. They do not have a budget surplus.

Investing Our Money

In 1989, Kim purchased her first rental property. She put down $5,000 and made $25 in positive cash flow per month. Today, Kim controls a multimillion-dollar portfolio and over a thousand rental units, and it's still growing. If we had not made investing an expense and paid ourselves first, we might still be paying everyone else first.

SAVINGS

We saved money until we had over a year's expenses in cash. Instead of holding cash in a retail bank, we hold it in gold and silver ETFs (exchange-traded funds). This means that if we need cash, i.e., liquidity, our liquid assets are held by our stockbroker in gold and silver certificates, not in cash at a retail bank. As you know, I do not like the U.S. dollar, because it continues to drop in value. Holding cash, or savings, in gold and silver also hinders me from spending it. I hate cashing in gold and silver for dollars. That's trading an asset that rises in value for a commodity that depreciates.

GOD IS OUR PARTNER

As far as tithing goes, we continue to donate a large percentage to charitable organizations. It's important to give. As my very religious friend says, "God does not need to receive, but humans need to give." Also, the reason we give is because tithing is our way of paying our partner—God. God is the best business partner I've ever had. He asks for 10 percent and lets me keep the other 90 percent. You know what happens if you stop paying your partners? They stop working with you. That is why we tithe.

COMING UP SHORT

When we budgeted for a surplus, the first thing Kim and I found out was that we were not earning enough money. One of the benefits of coming up short every month was that we faced the problem of not enough money early on, rather than later in life. I suspect there are many people who are coming up short every month and will come up short later in life when their working days are over. Then it might be too late to solve the problem of not having enough money.

As I stated at the start of this book, if you don't solve a problem, you will have that problem all your life. Problems rarely solve themselves. That is why we decided to pay ourselves first, early in life, even though we came up short. Coming up short forced us to solve the problem of not enough money.

WHO SCREAMS THE LOUDEST?

When we paid ourselves first, the people who screamed the loudest were the banks and people we owed money to. Instead of letting them intimidate us into paying them, we let them intimidate us into increasing financial IQ #1: making more money.

Many people do not pay themselves first because no one yells at them. No one hires a bill collector to collect from themselves. You do not threaten yourself with foreclosure. In other words, we do not put pressure on ourselves if we do not pay ourselves. Yet we bow to pressure from our creditors and pay them. Kim and I used the pressure tactics of our creditors from our expense column to motivate us to make more money and increase our income.

Budget Tip #2: The expense column is the crystal ball.
If you ever want to predict a person's future, just look at the person's discretionary monthly expenses. For example:

Person A	Person B
Donation to church	Six-pack of beer
Savings	New shoes
Book on investing	New TV
Seminar on investing	Football tickets
Gym dues	Six-pack of beer
Donation to charity	Bag of potato chips
Personal coach	Six-pack of beer

Rich dad said, "You can tell a person's future by looking at what they spend their time and money on." He also said, "Time and money are very important assets. Spend them wisely."

You can tell how important a budget surplus is to someone by looking at his or her expense column. For example:

Income Statement

Income
Paycheck (earned income)

Expense
Income taxes
Social Security taxes
401(k) pension contribution
Home mortgage
Car payments
Credit card bills
Food
Clothing
Gasoline
Electricity

Balance Sheet

Assets	Liabilities
	Home mortgage
	Car payments
	Credit card debt
	Retirement

Just look at how much money is being paid to other organizations or people first. Notice that I put retirement as a liability. In technical terms, it is an *unfunded liability*, until it becomes an asset. And if you are banking on your 401(k) for your retirement, you will be paying the highest percentage in taxes because it is taxed as earned income.

Compare that expense column to a *pay yourself first expense column.*

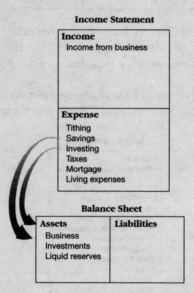

Income Statement

Income
Income from business

Expense
Tithing
Savings
Investing
Taxes
Mortgage
Living expenses

Balance Sheet

Assets	Liabilities
Business	
Investments	
Liquid reserves	

Remember this: your asset column is *your* column. If you do not pay yourself first, no one else will. Through your everyday expenses you and God, if you believe in and tithe to God, determine your financial future.

Budget tip #3: My assets pay for my liabilities. My poor dad believed in buying cheap. He thought being frugal was smart budgeting. We lived in an average house in an average neighborhood. My rich dad loved luxury. He lived in a fabulous home, in an affluent neighborhood, and lived an abundant lifestyle. He did not like being cheap, although he was still careful with his money.

If my poor dad wanted a luxury item, he simply denied himself the luxury of owning. He said, "We can't afford it." If my rich dad wanted a luxury item, he simply said, "How can I afford it?" And the way he afforded it was to create an asset in the asset column, an asset that paid for the liability. His financial statement looked like this:

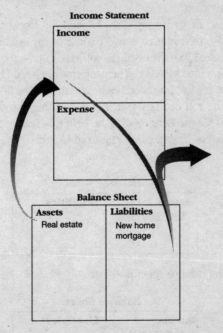

Income Statement

Income

Expense

Balance Sheet

Assets	Liabilities
Real estate	New home mortgage

In other words, he acquired assets by paying himself first. With the cash flow from the assets, he then purchased his luxury liabilities. If he wanted big luxuries, he first created big assets. What many people do is buy big luxuries first and never have enough money to purchase assets. Again, it's a matter of priorities.

The Bentley Account

Two years ago, I wanted a new car—a Bentley convertible. The price: $200,000. I had the money in my asset column. I could've purchased the car for cash. The problem with buying a $200,000 Bentley with cash is that the car is worth only $125,000 the moment I drive it off the lot. That is not a smart use of my cash.

Instead of spend my cash, I called my stockbroker Tom and authorized him to convert some of my gold and silver shares into $200,000 cash. His job was to take the $200,000 and turn it into $450,000. The project was named *The Bentley Account.* It took Tom about eight months, but he finally called and said, "You can buy your Bentley." I then wrote a check and paid for the Bentley with the cash that had been created by my assets. The transaction looked like this:

Starting balance-sheet position:

Balance Sheet

Assets	Liabilities
$200,000 cash	

Ending balance-sheet position:

Balance Sheet

Assets	Liabilities
$200,000 cash	Bentley

The reason I needed the account traded up to $450,000 is because the extra $50,000 was to offset the taxes on the capital gains and the commission that Tom made. At the end of the day, I had my Bentley, and I still had the original $200,000.

If I had just paid cash for the Bentley, without trading the account, the ending balance-sheet position would have looked like this:

Balance Sheet

Assets	Liabilities
	Bentley

I would have lost my $200,000 in cash assets (i.e., gold and silver certificates), and I would have lost an additional $75,000 due to the instant depreciation when I drove the car off the lot.

In the chapter on financial IQ #2: protecting your money, I wrote about how good brokers can make you rich and bad brokers make excuses. The Bentley Account is an example of a good broker making me rich and happy, allowing me to afford the luxuries of life. So, keep looking for a good broker if you don't already have one.

Assets = Luxury Liabilities

One of the benefits of being an author is that when I want a new liability, I first write a book, like this one, and the royalties from the book pay for the liability. The future transaction looks like this:

Balance Sheet

Assets	Liabilities
This book	Future liability

At this point it might be beneficial to remind you what an asset and a liability are. In my book *Rich Dad Poor Dad* I defined them as simply as this: An asset is something that puts money *in* your pocket. A liability is something that takes money *out* of your pocket. There is nothing wrong with enjoying liabilities—as long as you continue to pay yourself first and purchase them through the income generated by your assets. In the example above I used my assets to purchase my liability, and at the end of the day I still had my asset and my Bentley.

Examples of other assets' buying liabilities are shown in the diagram on page 105.

These are actual examples of how Kim and I use our desire for luxuries to make us richer, not poorer. As stated earlier, I do not believe in living below my means. I believe in first expanding my means and then enjoying life. A person with a low financial IQ only knows how to live below his or her means. In other words, cut expenses. If you do not give yourself the luxuries of life, why live life?

Balance Sheet

Assets	Liabilities
Apartment house	Permanent residence

Balance Sheet

Assets	Liabilities
Oil production	Beach house

Budget Tip #4: Spend to get rich. When the going gets tough, most people cut back rather than spend. This is one reason why so many people fail to acquire and maintain wealth.

For example, in the world of business, when a company's sales begin to drop, one of the first things the accountants do is cut back on spending. And one of the first things they cut back on is spending on advertising and promotion. With less advertising and promotion, sales drop, and the problem gets worse.

One sign of high financial intelligence is knowing when to spend and when to cut back. When Kim and I realized we were in trouble, instead of allowing our bookkeeper Betty to cut back and pay bills first, we went into full-scale sales, marketing, and promotion. We spent time, money, and energy increasing our income. We did not cut back on expenses.

In the workplace, there are many owners or managers who prey upon the weak—people who need their job and money. There are people who use the workers' weakness to make them weaker. For example, there are many big companies that cut your pay and/or increase your tasks to make you work harder. If you quit, they know that someone else will take your place. That is how the game is played.

That was the way things were at Xerox. When I did well, instead of give me a raise, they cut my territory, increased my quota, and cut my pay. It was their way of making me be more productive. At first I got very angry. I wanted to quit . . . and I almost did.

If not for my rich dad, I might have quit. Instead, rich dad pointed out to me that Xerox was training me in the ways of business. They were training me to do more with less. They were making me stronger. Once I saw the benefit to this way of business, I actually became a better businessperson. I learned to take the pressure and use it to my benefit.

When Kim and I told Betty the Bookkeeper to pay us first, before we paid our taxes and bills, it was our way of making us stronger, more viable for the world of business. Instead of crying, cringing, and paying when creditors called and threatened us, we used our creditors' energy to push us out the door to make more money.

When people criticize and tell lies to tear me down, I use their negativity to make me more positive and determined to win.

When problems arise, I use the problems to make myself smarter and to become bigger than the problem.

Take It One Day at a Time

Budgeting is a very important process to learn and be smart at. Take the process one day at a time. Instead of fighting about money, Kim and I used the process to discuss and learn more about money and ourselves. Positive things did not happen overnight, but they did happen. If you will sincerely work at creating a budget surplus, your life will become richer. That is what budgeting is about—using what you have, even if what you have is no money, to make you better, stronger, and richer.

How Being Poor Can Make You Rich

Again, the definition of a budget is: *a plan for the coordination of resources and expenditures*. You may notice this does not say a plan for the coordination of money. It's about the coordination of resources. A very important lesson from rich dad was that *a financial problem is a resource*—if you solve the problem. If you learn to take financial problems such as not enough money, a bad boss, or a mountain of debt, and use them as resources and opportunities to learn, you will slowly but surely create a budget surplus.

The lesson my rich dad taught me about financial intelligence is really about being resourceful. He taught his son and me to be resourceful and turn problems into opportunities. He said, "When I was a kid, I was poor. I am rich today because I saw being poor as an opportunity, a very important resource God gave me to use to become rich."

Good Debt and Bad Debt

There are two types of debt: good debt and bad debt. Simply said, good debt is debt that makes you richer and someone else amortizes (pays off) for you. Bad debt is debt that makes you poor, and that you have to amortize yourself.

Money causes some people to do goofy things. For example, many people do something financially insane, like buy a big house, put in a swimming pool, use credit cards to pay the bills, and then use the equity on their home to pay the credit card bills. This is an example of taking a bad situation and making things worse—creating a budget deficit.

Our government does the same thing. Many people in government think it takes money to solve problems, so the problems get bigger, requiring more money, which leads to a budget deficit.

A very serious problem in the world today is excessive bad debt. Bad debt is debt from a liability. Bad debt is a drag on countries, businesses, and individuals. One way to become rich is to see bad debt as an opportunity, a resource to make you richer, not poorer.

If bad debt is holding you back, then you may be your own worst enemy. When people borrow bad debt to solve problems, the problems definitely get worse and bigger. My suggestion is to look at the problem of bad debt as an opportunity to learn and grow smarter.

After one of my businesses failed, I lost nearly a million dollars. After selling off personal and company assets, I still owed about $400,000. To solve this bad debt problem, Kim and I came up with a plan to eliminate all of it. Once again, instead of cutting back, we instructed Betty the Bookkeeper to keep us on track and we used the problem to get richer, rather than poorer. In other words, we got richer while paying off all that debt. We continued to tithe, save, and invest, all while aggressively paying off all our bad debt.

(If you would like to know more about how Kim and I got out of bad debt, we created a CD called *How We Got Out of Bad Debt*, and a small accompanying workbook to guide those who are in bad debt. You can order it from our website, Richdad.com, for a nominal price plus shipping.)

Looking back at our mountains of bad debt, I am glad Kim and I grew smarter at budgeting through our problem-solving. While I never want to be that much in debt again, I am glad we learned from and solved the problem.

When Kim and I were short of money, we used that problem as a resource to make more money. Rather than live below our means, or borrow more bad money to pay for bad debt, we used our problems as resources to become re-sourceful, and as opportunities to learn and become richer.

Keep This in Mind

Financial IQ #3: budgeting your money, like financial IQ #2, is measured in percentages, the percentage of income that reaches your asset column.

If taking 30 percent of your income is too hard, then start with 3 percent. For example, if you earn $1,000, instead of allocating $300, or 30 percent, to your asset column, then direct 3 percent, or $30, towards your asset column. If this 3 percent makes life harder, that's good. A hard life is good if it makes you more resourceful.

The higher percentage you direct to your asset column, the higher your financial IQ #3. Today, Kim and I direct approximately 80 percent of our income directly into the asset column and do our best to survive on 20 percent. Also, we never say "we cannot afford it" and *we refuse to live below our means.* By continuing to keep things challenging, we become more resourceful, creating a more abundant life and a budget surplus.

Chapter 6

Financial IQ #4:
Leveraging Your Money

On August 9, 2007, the stock market plunged nearly 400 points. The Federal Reserve and central banks around the world began injecting billions in cash into the economy to make sure the panic did not spread.

The market was still nervous the next day. As I was getting ready for the day, a newscaster on a morning television program was interviewing three financial planners and getting their opinions. Their unanimous advice was, "Don't panic. Stay the course."

When asked for further advice, all three said, "Save money, get out of debt, and invest for the long term in a well-diversified portfolio of mutual funds." As I finished shaving, I wondered if these financial experts had all gone to the same school for parrots.

Finally, one advisor took a moment to say something different. She began by condemning the real estate market for causing the mess in the stock market, blaming greedy investors, unscrupulous real estate agents, and predatory mortgage lenders for causing the subprime mortgage mess, which led to the crash in the stock market.

This advisor said, "I told my clients that real estate was risky, and my advice has not changed. Real estate is a risky investment, and investors should invest for the long term in blue-chip stocks and mutual funds."

As the financial planner on television was ending her attack on real estate, my wife Kim walked into the room and said, "Remember we have a closing today on the 300-unit apartment house."

Nodding my head, I said, "I'll be there."

As I finished dressing, I thought, "It's funny, the financial advisor saying that investing in real estate is risky. The real estate markets are crashing at the same time Kim and I are buying a $17 million apartment house in Tulsa, Oklahoma . . . and we are excited about it. Are we on the same planet?"

The New Capitalism

On August 9 and 10, 2007, as investors lost billions of dollars, the U.S. Federal Reserve Bank was injecting billions of dollars into the banking system, doing its best to stop the panic in the real estate, stock, and bond markets. This injection of capital is an example of how the new capitalism operates, an economic system built on debt and manipulation by central bankers playing games with the world's money supply. It's almost like you and I using a credit card to pay our credit card bills.

Later that week, I was asked to be a guest on two television and three radio programs to comment on the crash. The hosts wanted to know what I thought about it, as well as what I thought about the Federal Reserve injecting cash into a crashing market, and whether the Federal Reserve Bank should save the market by lowering interest rates. In all of my interviews I said, "I don't like the central banks' manipulating the markets. I don't feel the government should bail out the rich hedge funds and financial institutions, shielding them from their own greedy mistakes." I also said, "I do feel for the little guy. In one day, millions of hardworking people, people who do not play games with money, watched their homes decline in value in the real estate market, their savings decline in value in the bond market, and their retirement portfolio decline in value in the stock market."

When asked if I was continuing to invest, I said, "Yes." When asked if I thought it was risky to be investing in crashing markets, I replied, "There is always risk." I then completed my thoughts by saying, "The ups and downs of markets do not affect *why* I invest or *what* I invest in."

Two Points of View

Although the question was not asked, I thought a better question might be, What is the difference between the financial planner who was negative on real estate and my point of view about investing in real estate? Or, Why, while so many people were panicking, was I excited about buying more property?

The answers to those questions are provided in this chapter through two financial concepts: *control* and *leverage*.

As stated repeatedly in this book, the rules of money changed after 1971 and 1974. There are new rules, and a new capitalism. In 1974, millions of workers began losing their paycheck for life, known as a defined benefit pension. They now had to save and invest for their retirement in defined contribution pension plans. The problem is most people have very little financial training or education in order to invest for their retirement properly. Another problem is the new rules of capitalism require workers to invest in assets they have *no control* and *no leverage* over. During market crashes, all most can do is watch helplessly as the financial hurricane whipsaws their wealth and financial security.

The new capitalism puts millions of workers' money into investments that allow them very little *control* or *leverage*. Because I have *control* over my investments, in this example a 300-unit apartment house, I am not as affected by market crashes. Because I have control, I am confident about using a lot more *leverage.* Due to control and leverage, I can achieve greater wealth, in less time, with very little risk, and minimize the effect of the booms and busts of markets on my investments.

The Market Has Been Crashing for a Long Time

As I wrote earlier, *USA Today* did a survey and found that the greatest fear in America was not terrorism, but the fear of running out of money during retirement. After August 9 and 10, 2007, I am sure that fear spread a little further.

The people who are worried have good reason to worry. When you look at the two charts below, you can see the effect of the rule changes of 1971 and 1974 on the value of the stock market. As you can see, the market has actually been crashing for a long time.

Dow in $ **Dow in Gold**

Just like housing, as the Dow is going up in price, its purchasing power is actually coming down. This loss of monetary purchasing power makes the financial future of most workers less secure. These charts say their future will cost them more money and become more expensive.

Without *leverage*, most workers cannot put enough money aside for their future, because the more money they save the less valuable it becomes. There is a funny story about the German economy just before Hitler came to power that illustrates this concept. The story goes that a woman took a wheelbarrow filled with money to the bakery to buy a loaf of bread. After negotiating a price for the bread, she came out of the bakery to get her money, only to find that someone had stolen her wheelbarrow and left her money. This is happening to the American saver.

How much will a retired person need in savings to afford retirement in such an inflationary economy? What happens if you are retired and need lifesaving surgery, which government medical programs will not pay for? What do you do if your problem is not having enough money to retire on?

This is why financial IQ #4: leveraging your money, is so important. Leverage makes your money work harder for you by using other people's money, *and* if you have a high financial IQ #3, you can pay less and less in taxes.

What Is Leverage?

In very simple terms, the definition of leverage is *doing more with less*. A person who puts money in the bank, for example, has no leverage. It's the person's money. A dollar in savings has a leverage factor of 1:1. The saver puts up all the money.

For my investment in the 300-unit apartment house, my banker put up 80 percent of the $17 million real estate investment. By using my banker's money, my leverage is 1:4. For every dollar I invest in the deal, the bank lends me four dollars.

So why did the financial planner on TV say that real estate

was such a risky investment? Once again, the answer is *control*. If an investor lacks the financial intelligence to control the investment, the use of leverage is very risky. Since most financial planners put people into investments where they have no *control*, they should not use *leverage*. Using leverage to invest in something you do not control would be like buying a car without a steering wheel and then stomping on the gas pedal.

Most of the people being hurt by the real estate meltdown are people who were counting on the real estate market to keep going up and increasing their home's value. Many people borrowed money against their inflated home value. Now their home may be worth less than what they owe. They have no control over the investment and are at the mercy of the market.

Many homeowners who still can make their mortgage payments feel bad because the value of their home has dropped. They watch the equity in their home disappear. When housing prices drop, many homeowners feel they have lost money. This is sometimes referred to as the *wealth effect*. Due to inflation, which is not really an increase in asset value but a decline in purchasing power of the dollar, many people feel wealthier as their home's value appears to increase. When they feel wealthier, they borrow more money (leverage) and spend more money on liabilities. This is a direct result of the new capitalism, an economic expansion based upon the decline of the dollar and an increase in debt.

My Worth Is Not Based upon Net Worth

The wealth effect is rooted in the illusion of net worth. Net worth is the value of your possessions minus your debt. When a house goes up in value most people feel their net worth has gone up. For those of you who have read my other books, you may already know that I feel net worth is *worthless*, for three reasons:

1. Net worth is often an estimate based upon *opinions*, not *facts*. The value of a home is only an estimate. You will not know the true price until the house is sold. This means many people overinflate their home's estimated value. Only when they sell their home will they know the facts: the real price and the real value. Unfortunately, many people may have already borrowed against the perceived value of their house and may owe more than they can sell the house for.

2. Net worth is often based upon possessions that have a declining value. When I fill out a credit application, I'm allowed to list most of my possessions in the asset column. I'm allowed to list my business suits, shirts, ties, and shoes as assets, just as I can list my cars. You and I know that a used shirt has very little value, and a used car has considerably less value than a new car.

3. Net worth going up is often caused by the dollar going down. Some of the appreciated value of a house is due to the decline in value of the dollar. In other words, the house is not going up in value. It just takes more dollars to buy the same house because the government and central banks keep injecting more funny money into the system to keep the economy afloat, and to keep the feel-good illusion of prosperity alive.

A Politician's Greatest Fear

The reason I used the words "feel-good illusion of prosperity" is because the greatest fear of politicians and bureaucrats is people feeling bad. Throughout history kings, queens, and rulers have been overthrown and even executed when the people *feel bad*. You may recall the French people chopped off the head of their queen, Marie Antoinette, and the Russian people executed the last czar, his wife, and his kids.

The old capitalism was based upon tough economic fundamentals. This new capitalism is based upon *feel-good economics*. As long as a person's net worth is going up, the illusion of prosperity, based upon debt, not production, continues. Who needs freedom when you've got things? As long as the world economy allows the U.S. government and the U.S. consumer to borrow and spend, the fairy-tale global economy will continue. If the dream turns into a nightmare and the feel-good bubble bursts, heads will roll again. They may not roll physically, but heads will roll politically, professionally, and financially.

Value Not Based upon Inflation

The value of my $17 million apartment house is not based upon inflation or the price of the building. While price is important, I am not counting on the price of the building going up due to some magical, unseen market condition. I am not counting on an increase in net worth to feel good, or worrying about a market crash and feeling bad. That is why the booms and busts of the markets do not concern me that much.

The value of my apartment house is based upon the rent my tenants pay. In other words, *the true value of the property is the value my tenants think the property is worth*. If a renter thinks the apartment is a good value at $500 a month, that *is* the property's value. If I can increase the perceived value of my property to my tenants, I, not the market, have increased the value of the property. If I increase rents without an increase in perceived value, the tenant moves to the community down the street.

The value of *rental real estate*, in this case my apartment houses, is dependent on jobs, salaries, demographics, local industry, and supply and demand of affordable housing. In a housing crash, the demand for rental units often goes up, which means demand and rents go up. If rents go up, the value of my *rental real estate* may go up, even if the value of *residential real estate* is coming down.

There are three specific reasons why I'm not concerned about market crashes when it comes to the purchase of my 300-unit apartment house. One reason is because Tulsa, Oklahoma, is an oil boomtown. High-paying jobs are plentiful. The oil industry needs workers, and transient workers need rental housing. The second reason is because a local college near the apartment house is doubling its number of students, but not the number of on-campus housing units, which increases demand for rental apartments. As many of you know, there is another baby boom commonly referred to as the echo boomers, a generation just now entering college, which is 73 million strong. A majority of them will be renters. The third reason is because the fixed interest rate on the existing loan is very low. Low interest payments, lower expenses, and increasing income will increase property value, not market fluctuations.

This means the 300-unit apartment house offers me both *control* and *leverage*. My job as an investor on this apartment house is to increase my leverage from 1:4 to possibly 1:10— i.e., doubling the value of the property through operations, not the market. I can do this as long as I have control.

Leverage Is Not Risky

Many financial advisors will tell you that higher returns mean higher risk. In other words, leverage is risky. That is absolutely false. Leverage is risky only when people invest in assets that they have no control over. If a person has control, leverage can be applied with very little risk. The reason most financial advisors say that higher returns mean higher risk is simply because they sell only investments that allow very little control.

As mentioned above, my $17 million apartment house in Tulsa is a good investment to use leverage with because I have control over the operations, and the operations (i.e., the amount of income that is collected through rents) determine the value of the investment. A house is not a good investment, and leverage is risky with a house because you do not control the value of the house. The value of a house is based on the market and the purchasing power of the currency it was purchased with. These things are out of your control.

What Is Control?

The major flaw in paper assets such as savings, stocks, bonds, mutual funds, and index funds is the *lack* of control. And because you have no control, it is difficult and risky to apply leverage. Because these paper assets offer very little control, it is difficult to get a bank to lend you any money to invest in these assets. So, what is control?

The diagram of the financial statement illustrates four of the main controls a professional investor and a banker want.

Income Statement

| **Income** |
| Sales |
| Rents |
| |
| |
| **Expense** |
| Operational costs |
| |
| |

Balance Sheet

Assets	**Liabilities**
Business	Debt
Real estate	

As an entrepreneur, I have control over the four columns in the financial statement of my business. As a real estate investor, I also have control over the four columns of the financial statement of my investment.

Financial Intelligence Is the Key to Control

Financial intelligence is the key to control. Financial intelligence increases control, and financial IQ measures the financial returns of financial intelligence. Take the 300-unit Tulsa apartment house as an example:

1. The income column. The first step after acquiring the property is to increase the rent. The property is already profitable and cash flows with existing rents. In other words, I am already making money from day one. Even so, the objective or business plan is to raise the rent per unit an additional $100 a month over the next three years by the following means:

1. Raising the existing rents that are under market.
2. Installing washers and dryers in all the units and charging extra for rent.
3. Completing improvements to the property like landscaping and new paint.

All of these can be completed by using the bank's money, not mine. When we provided the bank our business plan, these improvements were part of it, and were factored into the total loan amount. Multiplying 300 units by $100 over three years, this increases the entire project's monthly income by $30,000 a month, or an additional $360,000 a year. This increase in income is an example of control and leverage.

If the plan works, three years from now my financial IQ #4 (leverage) will be infinite because the increase in income will be achieved by no additional capital from investors, just good knowledge of how to manage the asset (control) to higher and higher profitability. The increase in financial IQ is *infinite* because the increase in income will be achieved using investor control and the bank's money.

2. *The expense column.* The next controllable objective is to lower expenses. This is done in different ways. One specific example is by reducing labor costs through reduced administrative costs. Since we own other properties, many costs can be brought back to the main company. These are sometimes called "back-office expenses." They are the cost of accountants, bookkeepers, attorneys, and administrative staff. Other expenses that can come down are insurance, property taxes, water consumption, maintenance, and landscaping through better cost management and economy of scale. Also, expenses can be reduced and income can go up by keeping turnover low, the time it takes to re-rent an apartment. For example, the moment a tenant informs the management company that he or she is leaving, an ad is run advertising the apartment's availability. Once vacated, the cleaning crew comes in that day, and the apartment is ready to show to a potential new tenant that night. And in many cases, an apartment is rented before the existing tenant even moves out.

Obviously, many incompetent investors fail to reduce expenses and actually increase them, making the property a bad investment—for them. Often, they fail to manage the quality of tenants and the attractiveness of the property because they are trying to save money. In most cases, the property goes down in value. It's these poorly run properties that we like to buy because we can turn them into good investments through good property management. In other words, we make good money from bad investors.

Property Management Is a Key Control

As you know, property management is one of the keys to profitability of real estate. Property management is a key control. Like most investors, I hate property management. That is why I have Ken McElroy, author of *The ABC's of Real Estate Investing*, as a partner. His company is absolutely the best. If you would like more information on property management or how to increase the value of real estate through property management, The Rich Dad Company offers several books and audio products created by my friend and investment partner Ken, whose company is a leading property management company in the southwestern United States.

One of the reasons why I stay clear of most stocks and mutual funds is because I have no control over expenses—especially management salaries, bonuses, and fees. It makes me sick to read about a greedy CEO's increase in pay, even as shareholder value drops. For example, Robert Nardelli, CEO of Home Depot, was being paid $38 million a year in salary, plus a guaranteed $3 million bonus each year. Unfortunately, things didn't go well and Nardelli finally resigned, but only after the board of directors agreed to pay him $210 million to do it.

To me, this is excessively expensive, and a rip-off. It's why I don't like paper assets. Most paper assets are run by MBAs, employees who think more about their personal finances than their investors' financial security. By the way, Home Depot's executive compensation, while high, is not necessarily an exception. It's the norm.

3. The liability column. My 300-unit apartment house had an existing mortgage interest rate of just 4.95 percent. The low interest rate increases the asset value of the entire property. By adding a second mortgage at 6.5 percent, we created a blended rate of about 5.5 percent (taking into account the different amounts of the two loans). This low interest rate is an important control and leverage. A percentage point on millions of dollars has a great impact on net income.

For example, a 1 percent savings on a $10 million mortgage is $100,000 in extra income annually. As the diagram on the bottom of this page illustrates, reducing debt and interest rate expense on debt is also an example of leverage.

4. *The asset column.* By increasing rents, reducing expenses, and reducing debt, or interest on debt, the asset value of the property increases.

As you can see by the financial statement diagram on the top of page 125, having controls and getting numbers to move in the desired direction are a form of leverage, and a function of financial intelligence.

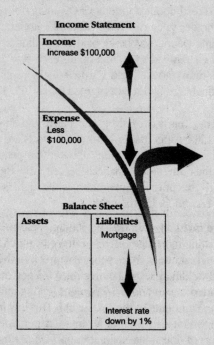

Income Statement

Income
Increase $100,000

Expense
Less
$100,000

Balance Sheet

Assets

Liabilities
Mortgage

Interest rate
down by 1%

Income Statement

Income
Income up due to:
1. Increased rents
2. Reduced expenses
3. Reduced mortgage costs

Expense

Balance Sheet

Assets	Liabilities
Asset value up due to:	
1. Increased rents	
2. Reduced expenses	
3. Reduced mortgage costs	

Bobbing for Apples

Today, with the ups and downs of the market, many investors look like old-time carnivalgoers who bobbed for apples floating in a tub of water. It looks like fun, but it's not something I want to do every day just to make a buck.

Rather than watching the price of my stock or mutual funds bob up and down in the market, I want control over my financial statement. By having the financial intelligence to control income, expenses, debt, and ultimately the value of my investment, I have control over my financial destiny.

The investor has no control and no leverage power in any of the four columns of the financial statement with savings, stocks, bonds, mutual funds, or index funds.

A Pause before Going On

Before going on into higher forms of leverage and control, I believe it is important to recap and review the points covered so far, before getting more complex. These are the seven points:

Point #1: There are many types of leverage. The financial leverage most people are familiar with is the leverage of debt, a.k.a. OPM, other people's money. There are other types of financial leverage, such as the leverage of financial intelligence applied to financial controls. In fact, all five financial intelligences, which are increasing income, protection from predators, budgeting, leverage, and information, are forms of leverage. Leverage is anything that makes your job a little easier. It's easier to move a heavy object with a forklift, and it's easier to make a sophisticated investment decision with a higher financial IQ.

Point #2: Most investors invest in paper assets, assets they have very little control over. Examples of paper assets are savings, stocks, bonds, and mutual and index funds. Because these assets allow little to no control, these investors have very little leverage and low returns on investment, and reflect a low financial IQ. An example of low financial IQ is a 5 percent return on savings, paying taxes on that return, and then having inflation almost wipe out its value.

Point #3: An increase in returns does not mean an increase in risk. When financial advisors say that an increase in returns means an increase in risk, they are right when speaking about paper assets. They are wrong when speaking for all assets.

Assets such as a business or real estate require more financial intelligence, allow for more financial control, and permit a higher degree of leverage with very low risk. *The key to low risk is higher financial intelligence.* This is why I recommend that people start small and stay small, as they allow their financial intelligence to increase. With an increase in financial intelligence, their returns on their investments increase. If financial intelligence is low, then leverage may deliver a blow to financial IQ, the measured returns on the investments.

Point #4: *Most financial advisors are not investors.* Financial advisors are simply salespeople. Most financial advisors, even many real estate brokers, invest only in paper assets, if they invest at all. Most have very little leverage professionally and financially. In many cases, their professional and financial leverage ratios are 1:1. A 1:1 professional ratio means they get paid for their work, and only their work—a day's pay for a day's work.

As a business owner, I have thousands of people working to assist me. As an investor, like in the example of the Tulsa apartment house, I have 300 tenants helping me pay for my investment, the bank lending me four dollars for every one of my dollars, and the tax department giving me tax breaks on my income. These are examples of different types of leverage.

Point #5: *Financial education increases financial intelligence.* Most people invest in paper assets such as savings, stocks, bonds, and mutual and index funds because they do not need or want control. All they want is to turn their money over to an investment advisor who hopefully does a good job. Out of sight, out of mind. If people want more control, the first thing they need to control is their financial education, which increases their financial intelligence and hopefully increases their financial controls and leverage ratios.

Point #6: *Leverage can work in two ways.* Leverage can make you rich and leverage can make you poor. This is why leverage requires financial intelligence and financial controls.

With stocks, a trader can use the leverage of options. If a trader thinks the market is going up, the trader may use a call option, which is the right to purchase a stock at a certain price within a certain time. For example, if the stock is $10 today and the trader senses the price will go higher, the trader may buy a call option for $1. If the trader is correct, and the stock goes to $20, the trader has made $10 with $1. If the trader thinks the market is going down, the trader may use a put option, or short the stock.

In other words, a trader has the potential to make money if the stock price is going up or going down. The problem, however, is that the trader has no control over the asset, just control over the terms of their trade. As expected, most financial advisors who sell mutual funds and recommend diversification say that trading a stock is risky—and it is for those who lack training and experience.

Learning to trade a market, even in real estate, is an important part of an investor's financial education. Real estate investors also use options. In real estate a call option is known as a down payment. If you are a flipper, a down market in real estate can be disastrous.

Since most of my investment in real estate is based upon rental prices and operating costs of a property, up and down markets in real estate do not affect me as much. While I do occasionally flip a property, especially if someone is willing to pay me a ridiculous price for it, as a practice I would rather buy a property and collect rent and other income for a long time. Then I look for another property to buy and hold.

For those who are interested in learning about investing in up and down markets, we have our board game *CASHFLOW 202*, a game that teaches you to trade with play money. *CASHFLOW 202* is an addition to *CASHFLOW 101*. It is strongly recommended you start with *CASHFLOW 101* before moving on to *CASHFLOW 202*.

There are CASHFLOW Clubs all over the world for people who want to learn the games before purchasing them. Financial education is essential for anyone wanting to use more leverage.

Point #7: When most financial advisors recommend diversification, they are not really diversifying. There are two reasons why the diversification they recommend is not diversification. The first reason is that financial advisors invest in only one category of asset: paper assets. As the market crash of August 9 and 10, 2007, revealed, diversification did not protect paper asset values. The second reason is that a mutual fund is already a diversified investment. It is a hodge-podge of good and bad stocks. When a person buys several mutual funds, it is like taking several multivitamins. When a person takes multiple multivitamins, the only thing that goes up in value is the person's urine.

Professional investors don't diversify. As Warren Buffett says, "Diversification is a protection against ignorance. Diversification is not required if a person knows what they are doing."

My rich dad would say, "Whose ignorance are you protecting yourself against, your ignorance, your advisor's ignorance, or your combined ignorance?"

Instead of diversify, professional investors do two things. One is to focus only on great investments. This saves money and increases returns. The second is to hedge. Hedging is another term for insurance. For example, my 300-unit apartment house is required by the bank to have all sorts of insurance. If the property burns down, insurance pays my mortgage and rebuilds the building. Best of all, the cost of the insurance is paid out of the rental income itself.

Two of the main reasons I do not like mutual funds is that banks do not lend money on them and insurance companies will not sell me insurance against catastrophic loss if the market crashes—and all markets crash.

On to More Leverage, Higher Returns, and Lower Risk

Focus, not diversification, is the key to more sophisticated leverage, higher returns, and lower risk. Focus requires more financial intelligence. Financial intelligence begins with knowing what you are investing for. In the world of money, there are two things investors invest for: capital gains and cash flow.

1. Capital gains. Another reason so many people think investing is risky is because they invest for capital gains. In most cases, investing for capital gains is gambling, or speculation. When a person says, "I'm buying this stock, mutual fund, or piece of real estate," he or she is investing for capital gains, an increase in the price of the asset. For example, if I had purchased the $17 million apartment house hoping I could sell it for $25 million, then I would be investing for capital gains. As many of you know, investing for capital gains means a tax increase in some countries.

2. Cash flow. Investing for cash flow is a lot less risky. Investing for cash flow is investing for income. If I put savings in the bank and receive 5 percent in interest, I am investing for cash flow. While interest is low-risk, the problem with savings is the return is low, taxes can be high, and the dollar keeps losing value. When I purchased the 300-unit apartment house, I was investing for cash flow. The difference is I was investing for cash flow using my banker's money for a higher return on investment and paying less in taxes. That is a better use of leverage.

What Are You Investing For?

Most financial advisors recommend that a person invest in growth funds when he or she is young. Investing for growth is investing for capital gains. They advise older investors to then shift their growth funds into income funds or annuities. In other words, invest for cash flow when you are older. They believe cash flow is less risky and more certain.

Three Types of Investors

When it comes to capital gains or cash flow, there are three general types of investors. They are:

1. Those who invest only for capital gains. In the world of stocks these people are called *traders*, and in the real estate market they are called *flippers*. Their investment objectives are generally to buy low and sell high. When you look at the CASHFLOW Quadrant, traders and flippers are actually in the S quadrant, not the I quadrant. They are considered professional traders, not investors. On top of that, in America, traders and flippers are taxed at the higher S quadrant tax rates and do not enjoy the benefits of the tax breaks the I quadrant receives.

2. Those who invest only for cash flow. Many investors like savings or bonds because of the steady income. Some investors love municipal bonds because they pay a tax-free return. For example, if an investor buys a tax-free municipal bond paying 7 percent interest, the effective return on investment (ROI) is the same as receiving a 9 percent taxable return.

In real estate, many investors love triple net leases (NNN). With NNNs investors receive income without the expenses of taxes, repairs, and insurance. The tenant covers those costs. In many ways, a triple net lease is like a municipal bond, because a lot of the income can be tax-free or tax-deferred.

While I love triple net properties, as expected, the trouble is finding a good property with a good tenant willing to pay a high return. Today, as I write, most NNN properties are only paying about a 5 percent to 6 percent return. Not that exciting. The good news is that if I dig deeper, which I will go into later, I might be able to find a property with a much higher return, all the while using more leverage and my bank's money to lower my risk, which is why I prefer triple net real estate over tax-free municipal bonds. This leads us to the third type of investor.

3. *The investor who invests for capital gains as well as cash flow.* Years ago, old-time stock investors invested for both capital gains and cash flow. Old-timers still talk about the price of a stock going up as well as paying the investor a dividend. But that was in the old economy, the old capitalism.

In the new capitalism, most paper investors are looking for the quick buck, to make a killing. Today, the big investment houses are hiring the smartest whiz kids out of college and using the power of supercomputers and computer models to look for the slightest market patterns they can exploit. For example, if the computer picks up a 1 percent differential, let's say in tech stocks, the investment house will bet millions of dollars, hoping to gain 1 percent on millions of dollars in a few hours. This is very high leverage, and very risky.

These computer models also cause a lot of the volatility in the markets and often cause crashes. When the stock market announces that program trading has been halted, it is talking about these computer programs' being halted. The markets crash if the computers say *sell*. If the computers say *buy*, the markets boom, and then they crash. In other words, prices can go up or down for no fundamental or business reason at all. A stock price may have no relationship to the value of the company because the computers created an artificial supply or demand. If you recall the dotcom era, companies that were not companies, but rather just good ideas, were valued at billions of dollars, and companies that were really valuable had their share prices trashed when the dotcom boom busted.

As an old-time investor in this new era of capitalism, I must be smart enough to invest for capital gains, cash flow, leverage of debt, and tax advantages, as well as be above the turmoil the whiz kids and supercomputers cause in the marketplace.

For instance, I recently purchased a stock, even though I do not have control, because the company, an old boring Industrial Age company, historically pays a steady 11 percent dividend. When the share price dropped in the recent market crash, I bought the stock because the price of the cash flow became cheaper. So I do occasionally buy paper assets, but I tend to buy for cash flow. Being a little guy and not having control over the company, I do not use leverage. I only invest with cash I can afford to lose if I'm wrong. If this particular stock goes up in price, I may sell because I like investing for both cash flow and capital gains. My ROI, *return on investment*, goes up if and when I can receive both cash flow and capital gains.

There are three components to being a good real estate investor. They are:

1. *Good partners.* As Donald Trump says, "You cannot do a good deal with bad partners." This does not mean bad partners are bad people. They may just be bad or wrong partners for you. For this 300-unit apartment house project to work, I must be sure I have good partners. My partners are my wife, Kim; Ken; and Ross. We have done many deals together and have made a lot of money. We have also run into many problems, and in solving the problems have become smarter and better partners.

2. Good financing. Real estate is primarily a function of financing. Many people say, "Location, location, location." I say, "Financing, financing, financing." If you can secure good financing, the deal works. If you have bad financing, the deal will not. To illustrate my point, let's say the seller says, "I want $35 million for my $17 million apartment complex." If the seller lets me finance the $35 million purchase price at $1 a month for 30 years with a balloon payment of $35 million at the end of the term, I would take the deal and give the seller the asking price. At $1 a month for 30 years, I can afford to pay $35 million for a $17 million property. As they say in the world of finance, "I'll give you your *price* if you will give me my *terms*."

I know some of you think $35 million is just an extremely ridiculous example. It actually is not. In the world of finance, paying ridiculous prices is pretty common. It is often just a matter of who the buyer and seller are and their ability to use the power of finance to achieve their goals.

For example, a few years ago, a piece of property came up for sale near my office. When I asked the broker what the price was, he said $2 million. I laughed, said he was joking, and left. At best, I thought the property was worth $750,000. Today, a major hotel chain is putting a flagship property on that piece of dirt. I do not know what that piece of dirt is worth today, but it is definitely more than $2 million. As my friend Ken McElroy says, "The person with the better plan wins." And as Donald Trump says, "Think big." Every time I drive past that property, I say to myself, "Think bigger."

3. Good management. One of the reasons for my confidence in the $17 million, 300-unit property is that I have good partners. Ken owns a property management company, and his partner Ross owns a real estate development company. In the following paragraphs, I will further explain how property management and development are essential to increasing rents, lowering expenses, and increasing asset value.

If I had bad partners, bad financing, and bad management, the 300-unit apartment deal would be a financial disaster. If I were the only one investing, I would not invest. It is too big and complex a project.

Having *control* over these three components—good partners, good financing, and good management—I am more willing to use debt as *leverage*. Without control, I would probably *not* use debt financing. If there is higher risk, such as speculating in a stock or a commodity, I like to use only money I can afford to lose.

Higher Returns with Less Risk

I'm going to further explain my confidence in the investment (thanks to my partners and having control over the 300-unit apartment project), why I am willing to use a lot of leverage, why I believe the risk is low, how I make more money, and how I pay less in taxes. There are three more advanced investment strategies, investment strategies that require a higher level of financial intelligence. The three advanced leverage strategies are OPM, ROI, and IRR.

1. OPM: Other people's money. There are many ways to use OPM. With the 300-unit apartment building, I am using 80 percent leverage. First of all, the beauty of using the bank's money is that it is tax-free money. The other benefits of the bank's money are:

	Me	Bank
1. Appreciation	100%	0%
2. Income	100%	0%
3. Tax benefits	100%	0%
4. Amortization	100%	0%

As you can see from these numbers, the bank puts up 80 percent of the money but I receive 100 percent of the benefits. What a great partner.

2. ROI: Return on investment. A confusing concept for many investors is the return on their money, or ROI. For example, when you read financial publications, many mutual funds claim they have gone up by 10 percent. But my question is, did any of that 10 percent return to the investor? And how did they measure that 10 percent? Some funds measure the 10 percent by the price of the shares in the fund going up. For example, if a year ago the price per share in the fund was $10 and today it's $11, they can claim a 10 percent return. In this case the return was measured in capital gains.

As an investor who invests for both capital gains and cash flow, the only return I count is the cash flow. For example, if I invest $10 and each year after taxes I put $1 in my pocket from cash flow, my return is 10 percent. I do not count the return on asset appreciation because it is an estimate and does not become a reality unless I sell the asset.

The difference is that one measure of the ROI is in the price of the stock, and the other measure of ROI is money in my pocket. I actually want both, 10 percent in asset appreciation and 10 percent cash in my pocket. But cash flow is the only return that can be tangibly measured while I hold the asset.

Matching 401(k) Contributions with One's Own Money

Another confusing point is that financial planners claim companies match your retirement fund contributions. If the match is dollar-for-dollar up to a certain percentage, the advisor may claim that this is 100 percent ROI. That is not how I see it. My way of looking at matching contributions is that the company is simply putting my money in with more of my money. In other words, the contribution the company withholds and then contributes is still *my money*. It is money the company should have paid me anyway. It is part of my total compensation, an expense to the company.

When I talk about leveraged returns, I am talking about someone else's money . . . not my money.

More Leverage, Higher Returns

The reason leverage is so important is because the higher the leverage, the higher the return. For example, if I buy a $100,000 rental unit with my money, and I receive $10,000 a year net income, my cash-on-cash return is 10 percent. If I borrow $50,000 and am still able to receive a $10,000 return, my cash-on-cash return is 20 percent. If I finance the entire $100,000, and still receive a $10,000 return, my return is infinite. Infinite returns mean money for nothing. Ten thousand dollars flows into my pocket, and nothing comes out. The renters cover my expense, and I receive the income.

Money for Nothing

In my next example, again using the 300-unit apartment house, I will explain how I receive an infinite return by using leverage. The way this will be done is by raising rents and adding washers and dryers to each of the 300 units. This is how the numbers work in oversimplified terms:

Income Statement

Income
$50 increase in rent
$50 increase in rent due to washers and dryers

Expense
$10 a month in payments for the washers and dryers

Balance Sheet

Assets	Liabilities
	$1,000 debt to pay for the washers and dryers, and rehab of unit

The net $100-a-month increase in rents is due to increased rents to match the competition, upgrades to the exterior, and fitting each unit with washers and dryers.

This $100-a-month increase in income is a 100 percent financed transaction. We get extra money from the bank to do the renovations. We have the control. The increase in debt is more than covered by our increase in income. This extra $100 is technically an *infinite return* because all the expense is fronted by the bank, and all the returns come to me.

The increase of $100 per month is multiplied by 300 units. This is an increase in gross income of $30,000 a month, and $360,000 a year on top of the cash flow we are already getting.

This $360,000 is an infinite return, measured by cash flow in hand, not some fictitious capital gain on paper.

In summary, the bank puts up 100 percent of the money for these improvements and we receive the increase in income. The tenants pay for expenses and the mortgage.

3. IRR: *Internal rate of return.* One of the more complex, sophisticated, and often confusing measures of ROI is the internal rate of return. If investors really know what they are doing, they can increase their ROI by understanding IRR. The following diagram explains as simply as possible this more advanced way of measuring true investor returns.

Income Statement

Income Passive income
Expense Depreciation

Balance Sheet

Assets Appreciation	Liabilities Amortization

In overly simplified terms, internal rate of return (IRR) measures the other returns and other leverage that a well-controlled investment can provide.

1. *Income column: Passive income*. Most people understand that gross rents are part of the income column. Yet IRR also measures other forms of income. Passive income is subject to lower tax rates than earned income. In the U.S., passive income is not subject to Social Security or self-employment taxes. In other words, these taxes do not show up as expenses in the expense column, which is technically a gain in income.

2. *Expense column: Depreciation*. In the U.S., the tax department gives some investors an additional income that actually looks like an expense. This income is known as *depreciation*. Another term for depreciation is "phantom income." The reason it is phantom income is because it's income that shows up somewhere else. For example, let's say my tax bill is $1,000. The IRS may allow me to depreciate my investment by $200, allowing me to pay only $800 in taxes. This additional $200 is phantom income, or money I did not have to pay. It is $200 that remains in my pocket instead of going to the government.

   Depreciation is allowed for such things as refrigerators, ceiling fans, carpet, furniture, and other items that decline in value with age. A tax accountant can explain this to you if you own a business or real estate. There is no such thing as depreciation for paper asset investors.

3. *Liability column: Amortization*. Another form of income to the investor is known as amortization, which is a fancy word for paying off debt on a scheduled basis. When you have good debt, debt that someone

else such as a renter pays for you, amortization becomes income to you. In other words, as a tenant pays down my debt, that payment is technically income to me, income that is paid to reduce my debt as my cash stays in my pocket, ready for the next great investment opportunity to come my way. Additionally, while my tenant is paying down my debt, I still receive all the tax benefits associated with my investment.

4. *Asset column: Appreciation.* Appreciation is the increase in asset value. This is also income to you. This is not appreciation based upon some appraiser's idea of an increase in sales price based on comparative sales in the area. The way I measure appreciation is by the actual increase in income to my income column. For example, the increase of $360,000 in income from my 300-unit apartment house is measurable.

This is not an exact method for defining IRR, but it gives you an idea of how an investor can increase his or her return on investment far higher than most investors can receive from paper assets. At least you have an idea of what an IRR is. I would guess 95 percent of investors have never heard of internal rate of return. So you are now smarter and sharper than 95 percent of the investors out there.

The Exit Strategy

The beauty of the exit strategy on the 300-unit apartment house is once again the use of leverage to become even richer. Instead of selling the property and facing substantial capital gains taxes on the profit, we pull out the money by refinancing. We are able to do this because we have increased the value of the property through our improvements and management. The bank recognizes this increase in value and we are able to borrow against it. By leveraging the property's value, we pull money out of the property tax-free, and the improved operations more than cover the higher mortgage payment through higher income. By borrowing rather than selling, we get our down payment back, tax-free, and we get to keep the asset. At this point, the property's income is an infinite return because we have no money invested in the deal, yet we receive the income. This is the ultimate leverage.

Let's say after five years we are able to refinance the property and pull out $4 million tax-free. The numbers are in the diagram on page 143.

The $4 million refinanced dollars go to the investors, and pay back all initial equity and then some. Even better, we still maintain control over the 300 units, and the increased mortgage payment of $280,000 is paid for by the $360,000 increase in income.

The $360,000 increase in rental income, minus $280,000 in increased interest expense, leaves a net $80,000 in passive income. This $80,000 is an infinite return because the investors have received back their initial investment, yet still receive cash flow. It is free money. The investors get $4 million back and move on to purchase another apartment house.

Income Statement

Income
$360,000 in increased income
$4 million tax-free

Expense
$280,000 in additional interest payments at 7% interest

Balance Sheet

Assets	**Liabilities**
Apartment house	$4 million in extra debt

This is an example of using *control* and *leverage*. This is an example of getting rich according to the rules of the new capitalism, capitalism based on the use of debt to become richer. Rather than work hard to get out of debt, as those who follow the rules of old capitalism do, we work hard to find ways to get into more *good* debt and use more leverage.

Starting with Nothing

To some of you a $17 million, 300-unit apartment building sounds like a big investment. To some of you, it's a small investment. Ten years ago, buying a 300-unit apartment seemed big to Kim and me. Ten years from now, I am certain it will seem like a small investment. Kim, Ken, and

I are already planning much bigger projects to take on. Donald Trump and I are looking at a massive project not far from my home, a project we will break ground on in ten years.

I mention the size and dollar amounts of projects to make three points:

1. Being born poor and financially uneducated does not mean you cannot become rich. Very few people are born rich enough to buy a $17 million apartment complex. And no one is born smart enough to acquire, finance, and manage a 300-unit apartment complex by themselves. In other words, not having any money or financial education isn't an excuse not to get started. Yet billions of people let the problem of not having money or enough education stop them from becoming rich. They fail to take the first step. And if they *do* take the first step and then fail, make a mistake, lose money, or run into problems, many quit. That is why for billions of people, a $17 million project will always seem like a big project, a project bigger than their dreams.

2. Start small and take baby steps. In 1989, Kim's first investment was a $45,000 two-bedroom, one-bath home in Portland, Oregon. She put $5,000 down and made $25 a month. She was extremely nervous when she took her first step. Today, a $17 million apartment house is boring to her. She is ready for bigger projects.

In 1997 Ken McElroy started with a two-bedroom, two-bath condo in Scottsdale, Arizona. It cost $115,000, and he put down $23,000. He made $50 per month in cash flow. Today, he controls a real estate portfolio worth hundreds of millions of dollars.

I bought my first investment property in 1973. I had no extra money to invest. I was still in the Marine Corps and had just purchased my first home. Rather than let low pay and no money stop me, I signed up for a real estate investment course for $385. Within a few months I purchased my first investment property, a one-bedroom condo on the island of Maui, for $18,000. The property was in foreclosure, and the bank was desperate to get rid of the unit. The bank let me put the $2,000 down payment on my credit card. The property made me about $35 a month after paying my mortgage and credit card bill, which is an infinite return, since I borrowed 100 percent of the money. Once I proved to the bank that I could manage the property, it let me buy two more units. My investing career was launched.

About a year later, I sold the three properties for approximately $48,000 each and put nearly $90,000 in my pocket. Not a bad return on a $385 seminar and credit card down payments.

Even though I did it, I do not recommend that people use credit cards to make down payments. I do, however, recommend that a person read books and attend seminars before investing. One of the reasons The Rich Dad Company has intensive investment seminars is because I strongly believe in the power of our minds. Our minds are our most important form of leverage.

At our seminars, the instructors are fabulous. I must admit that they are better teachers than I am. They are much more focused and thorough with their content and delivery. They are well-trained, dedicated to your success, and, most importantly, they practice what they preach. Most students report that our courses open up their minds to a world of new opportunities, different ways of becoming financially free, and change their lives forever. You can find out more information on our website, Richdad.com.

3. Dream big. Most of us know that a child must be allowed to dream. The same is true for adults. As a couple, Kim and I have big dreams. Our dreams keep our marriage rich, young, and fun. Bigger investment projects keep us learning together, operating as a team, and growing together rather than growing apart. Instead of living below our means, we dream big, learn, and invest carefully in order to go beyond our means. It's not just about money . . . it's about life. Personally, Kim and I think it is a tragedy to live below your dreams.

In Conclusion

On August 9 and 10, 2007, as the markets of the world crashed, many people had no idea what the crash meant. Most people have no idea how it will affect their lives. Most people have no idea how the rule changes back in 1971 and 1974 have affected their lives.

Today, even in the richest country in the world, the U.S., millions of educated, hardworking people are earning less even if they are paid more, saving money that is losing value, clinging to their homes as their value declines, and using credit cards to pay their bills.

To make matters worse, because of a market crash, millions of educated, hardworking people think that investing is risky and to attain higher returns means you have to take on greater risks. There are only a few people who know that the key to *leverage* is *control*, and the key to control is financial intelligence.

The good news is that the higher your financial intelligence, the more money you make without needing money. In this new capitalism, it is truly possible to make *money for nothing*. In the Information Age, knowledge is the ultimate leverage. The more money you make without money, the higher your ROI and IRR, and the higher your financial IQ.

Since financial IQ is the numerical measure of financial intelligence, this means an *infinite return* means an infinite financial IQ. Tell that to your banker and financial planner the next time they tell you that 5 percent interest on savings, or 10 percent return on mutual funds, is a great return.

Chapter 7

Financial IQ #5: Improving Your Financial Information

In January of 1972, I was transferred from Camp Pendleton, California, to an aircraft carrier off the coast of Vietnam. It was my second trip to Vietnam. My first visit was in 1966. The Merchant Marine Academy sent students to sea for a year of study. My project was studying military cargo operations in a war zone—more specifically, how to safely load and unload bombs without killing ourselves. My second trip as a war pilot was a very different experience than studying the war as a student.

My primary job on board the carrier was as a helicopter gunship pilot. My primary mission was to fly as an escort for the larger troop helicopters. Our squadron was made up of mostly troop transport helicopters, the twin-rotor CH-46 and CH-53s, a.k.a. Jolly Green Giants. If the zone was hot with enemy fire, the job of the gunship was to protect the troop transport helicopters in the zone. Personally, I was happy to be a gunship pilot. It was a lot better than being a troop transport pilot. Transport pilots had to be extremely brave. They flew large helicopters into a hot zone, just sitting there as troops got on or off.

Top-Secret Job

My secondary job was as an assistant to the squadron's top-secret information officer. It was an extremely interesting job. For hours on end, we would sit, listen, observe, gather, and process top-secret information. At regular intervals during the day and the night, we gave briefings to the commanding officer and his team. Our job was to take raw data from the war and turn it into relevant information.

Life-or-Death Information

As an information officer, I gained a tremendous respect for information. Prior to Vietnam I never thought much about the subject. In school, I thought the study of information was a joke. To me, information was just data, mindless facts and figures, dates and times to be memorized in order to pass tests. In Vietnam, information was more important. It could mean life or death for my fellow pilots.

Today, I believe that I am a better entrepreneur and investor because of my position as information officer. Today, I know that information can mean life or death in war and the difference between being rich or poor in business.

Information More Important Than Life

In the process of preparing to go to Vietnam, we were trained to process infinite bits of information and be able to make split-second decisions under intense pressure. If we did a good job processing the information, we lived. If we didn't, we risked death. Once I realized that my life and the lives of others were dependent upon the quality of information I received, it became more important than even my own life.

In a previous book, I wrote about the first day I came under fire in Vietnam. I described the fear as well as the realization that the guy firing at me wanted to go home as much as I did. In the book, I related my crew chief's words of wisdom reminding me that in war there was no second place, no silver medal. It was gold or nothing. Watching real bullets screaming up at us, I realized school days were officially over. As we flew towards our death, years of training and information were being processed into one decision, one action. The good news is that my crew and I returned home that night. Sadly, the Vietnamese on the ground didn't. There was no second place.

The Most Important Asset

A friend of mine who is a Bible scholar often says, "Without knowledge, my people will perish." Today many people are perishing because they are without knowledge about money. We live in the Information Age. Even in very remote areas of the world, I have seen young people text messaging while at the same time riding the family's donkey cart. Never before has the entire world been so connected so quickly.

Information is the single greatest asset of this era. In previous ages, you owned factories, cattle ranches, gold mines, oil wells, or skyscrapers to be rich. In the Information Age, information alone can make you very rich. You don't need tangible resources like land, gold, or oil. The young entrepreneurs who created MySpace and YouTube have proved that. With just a few dollars, some information, and the leverage of technology, these twenty-year-olds have become billionaires.

Likewise, poor or mistaken information is a liability. Poor information creates poor people. One of the reasons so many people are struggling financially is simply because they have obsolete, biased, misleading, or erroneous information powering their most powerful asset, their brain. Many people who are struggling are doing so because they are using Industrial or Agrarian Age information in the Information Age. Examples of Industrial Age information are ideas such as, "I need a good education to get a high-paying job." An example of Agrarian Age information is, "Land is the basis of all wealth."

The Four Ages of Humanity

There have been four economic ages of humanity:

1. The Hunter-Gatherer Age. During this period nature provided the wealth. Tribes followed herds or searched for food. If you knew how to hunt and gather you survived. If you did not, you died. The tribe *was* social security. Socioeconomically, everyone was even. The chief didn't have a higher standard of living than the rest of the tribe. He may have eaten first and had more wives, but basically, fire was fire and a cave was a cave. In terms of money, there was only *one* class of people. Everyone was poor.

2. The Agrarian Age. Once humans learned how to plant seeds and domesticate animals, land became the wealth. Kings and queens owned the land, and everyone else worked on the land and paid a tax to the royals. That is why "real estate" strictly translated means *royal estate*. With the advent of domesticated animals, the royals rode horses and the peasants walked. That is why the word "peasant" is a derivative of many words broadly meaning *on the land and on foot.* Peasants owned nothing. Socioeconomically, there were *two* groups, the rich and the peasants.

3. The Industrial Age. In 1492, Christopher Columbus and other explorers went in search of trade routes, land, and resources. To me, that's when the Industrial Age really began. In the Industrial Age, resources such as oil, copper, tin, and rubber were wealth. During this era the value of real estate changed. In the Agrarian Age, land had to be fertile and able to grow crops or raise animals. In the Industrial Age, nonagricultural land became more valuable. For example, Henry Ford built his auto plant in Detroit because he could buy large tracts of rocky, unfertile, nonagricultural land for a great price. Today, industrial-use land has a higher value than agricultural land. Socioeconomically, a new class emerged, the middle class. There were now three groups of people: the rich, the middle class, and the poor.

4. *The Information Age.* This age officially started with the invention of digital computers. In the Information Age, information leveraged by technology is wealth, and very inexpensive and abundant resources, such as silicon, produce the wealth. In other words the price of getting rich has gone down. For the first time in history, wealth is available, affordable, and abundant for everyone, regardless of where he or she lives. Socioeconomically, there are now four groups of people: the poor, middle class, rich, and *super*-rich. Bill Gates is the most obvious example of the Information Age super-rich.

The Super-Rich

Today the super-rich can derive their wealth from any era. It's possible to be a super-rich hunter-gatherer as the Maori from New Zealand are from fishing rights. You can also be a super-rich rancher or farmer from the Agrarian Age, and be a super-rich automaker from the Industrial Age. As already mentioned, there are super-rich twenty-year-old billionaires of the Information Age, young people who became super-rich with the inexpensive and abundant resources of technology, information, and their ideas. The common bond among all these is that information enabled the coordination of resources at a much quicker and higher level than ever before. It is this coordination that creates the super-rich.

The Gap

At the same time, there are people who are perishing because of obsolete or inadequate information. There are indigenous tribes who are being wiped out as their forests are taken away. There are farmers going broke, and automakers laying off thousands of workers. Once-prosperous record store chains are now being wiped out by downloaded music.

In America, the richest country in the world, we have millions of people who are deeply in debt, clinging to the last strands of job security, and wondering how they will afford an education for their kids and a retirement for themselves. Millions struggle in this rich country because they continue to operate with Hunter-Gatherer, Agrarian, or Industrial Age ideas.

The widening gap between the super-rich and everyone else is made by information. The good news is that information is abundant and free. Today, it's relatively easy for a person, even the very poor or the young, to go from nothing to super-rich without much money. To be rich today, you do not have to be a conquistador, sailing to foreign lands and robbing the indigenous people of their resources. You do not need to raise millions of dollars in the stock market to build a car factory or employ thousands of workers. Today, information and a very inexpensive computer can transport you from poor to super-rich while you're sitting at home. All it takes is the right information.

Information Overload

So, the good news is that information is abundant and free. The bad news is that . . . information is abundant and free. The irony of the Information Age is that there is too much of it. Today, people complain about information overload. At any given moment a person can be watching television, surfing the Internet, and talking on the phone—while driving past digital billboards. In previous ages, no one complained about too much land or oil. Yet in the Information Age, people complain about having too much information and being overloaded with the very asset that could make them super-rich.

Military Intelligence

In Vietnam, I learned to respect the power of information. I became acutely aware of information's power to kill, as well as to save lives. Using military intelligence to kill no longer makes sense to me. Today, I prefer to use information to give life, not take it.

As an information officer I was also faced with information overload. While at war, the amount of information we had to process was staggering. Very quickly, we had to learn how to sort, categorize, discard, and process tremendous amounts of information from multiple and varied sources. If we didn't, we or others could die.

Classifying Information

To handle information overload, the military puts a great amount of effort into classifying information. Without classification, all information is equal and virtually worthless. As an information officer in Vietnam I learned to classify information according to a set of characteristics.

1. Time. In war and in business, information can be useful one minute and obsolete the next. War is fluid, always moving. So is business and investing. Enemy troops can be one place today and a hundred miles away tomorrow. In business, a business advantage can be priceless today and worthless tomorrow.

2. *Credibility.* We had to know who the information came from. Were our sources credible and reliable? Unfortunately, in the world of money, most people get their financial information from people they work with or salespeople—people who are struggling for money as well. They may be good, honest people, but they are not credible or reliable sources of financial information.

3. *Classification.* In the military, I learned to sort information into categories. For example, top-secret information was only available to those with top-secret clearances.

In the world of business and investing, top-secret or classified information is known as *insider information*. When the average investor hears the term, he or she thinks of illegal information . . . and sometimes it is. Insider information is illegal when a person receives information from someone inside a public company and uses it to buy or sell that company's shares.

In reality, all information is inside information. A more important question is, how far from the inside are you? By the time a person hears a hot tip about a company's new product or news that a company is in trouble, people on the inside and close to the inside have already traded on that information. The battle has already been won, and the average investor has lost.

Let me make it clear that I do not encourage or condone illegal insider trading on information. The distinction I want to make is about the importance of being on the inside and getting close to the information. One of the reasons I love being an entrepreneur and a real estate investor is because I am a legal insider who can trade on inside information. Since

I am not a public company, I can also freely tell my friends what I know and how I am investing.

In the stock market, professionals know that amateurs trade on ancient history. That is how professionals make their money. They make money from amateurs. An example is Mr. Average, an investor who gets up, reads the newspaper over a cup of coffee, and notices a news release from his favorite public company. He then calls his broker or goes online to make his trade. Even though the information may only be a few hours old, Mr. Average is already in a losing position. Mr. Average is late to the party because he was never invited. He is *not* on the inside. He is an outsider.

One of the main reasons rich dad encouraged me to develop my financial intelligence is so I could have access to inside information. The closer to the inside your information, the richer you become.

4. *Relative information.* Watching battlefield information change day by day, we as information officers were able to interpret *past* and *present* information to forecast *future* information. For example, if we knew that enemy troops were in one position on Tuesday, another position on Wednesday, and another position on Thursday, we could begin to predict where they were going and what their objectives might be. In other words, we had to know how information related to other information.

In the world of business and investing, this past, present, and future information gathering is known as watching the trends.

5. *Deceptive information.* In war, the enemy would often try to deceive us by sending deceptive information. They occasionally did this by using diversionary tactics. For example, they might move a large number of troops and equipment, making a lot of noise and dust, just to distract us from their real motives and objectives. Or they allowed us to capture one of their troops who provided erroneous information. Or they used a spy, someone we thought was on our side, to provide us with inaccurate information.

The Pump and Dump

Business and investing are rampant with deceptive information. An entrepreneur and investor must be constantly vigilant and on guard against deceptive information. For example, many times a financial expert will tell you something and then do the opposite. This person may go on television and say he is bullish on a stock and is buying it. This bit of information causes other people to buy the stock, driving the stock price up. Once the price is up, the person who recommended the stock sells and takes a huge profit. This is known as the *pump and dump.*

The Sleight of Hand

Another form of deception is known as the *sleight of hand*, a technique named after a magic trick. When a magician taps on his top hat, your eyes are drawn to the hat and away from what he is doing with his other hand behind his back.

In business, consumers are often deceived the same way. For example, a box of cereal may boldly say, "Low-Fat." A consumer worried about gaining weight thinks this is a good cereal for them. Upon closer inspection of the fine print, however, you find the cereal is low in fat but excessively high in sugar.

In investing, a mutual fund may advertise, "Highest returns of all funds." What the headline fails to state is that none of the other funds made any money and neither did their fund. It's like saying, "I caught the biggest minnow."

Classifying Information to Become Richer

There are a number of lessons I learned in the military about classifying information that are applicable to business:

Lesson #1: Facts vs. opinions. The key to military intelligence is to know the difference between facts and opinions. The same is true for financial intelligence. One of the reasons so many people think investing is risky is because they do not know the difference between facts and opinions. A few examples of opinions are:

- When someone says the shares of a company are going to go up, it's an opinion because it is about a future event.

- When someone says a person's net worth is a million dollars, it's an opinion because most valuations are opinions.

- If a person says, "He is very successful," this is an opinion because the definition of success is relative.

Lesson #2: Insane solutions. An insane solution occurs when a person uses information that is an opinion as a fact. In war this can kill you. In business it can ruin you. For example:

QUESTION: *"Why did you buy that house when you knew you couldn't afford it?"*

ANSWER: "I bought it because my broker said it was going to go up in value. I thought that I could buy the house, live in it, and then sell it for a profit, which would solve my money problems."

QUESTION: *"Why did you marry him even after you knew he was a womanizing lazy bum?"*

ANSWER: "Well, he was so cute. I was afraid I would lose him. I did not want anyone else to steal him from me. So even though I knew he fooled around and did not like to work, I thought that after we got married and had kids, I could change him."

QUESTION: *"Why did you stay at a job you hated for so many years?"*

ANSWER: "I thought I might get promoted."

QUESTION: *"Why do you invest in those mutual funds?"*

ANSWER: "Because my supervisor told me to. She said it was a good investment."

Lesson #3: Risky actions. In war, if you didn't verify information and acted on it blindly, you risked death. A risky investor invests based on opinions. Unfortunately, this describes most investors. Since most investors invest for capital gains, their investment decision is based upon *opinions* about the future. Many investors invest in mutual funds based upon the opinion that the stock market goes up 8 percent to 10 percent per year. If the opinion is wrong, they lose.

A smart investor knows the difference between facts and opinions. Generally a person who invests for capital gains is investing on an opinion. A cash flow investor invests for facts. If possible, a smart investor will invest using both opinion and facts, and invest for both cash flow and capital gains.

If you are investing in stocks, mutual funds, real estate, or business, ask yourself if the information you are basing your decision on is fact or opinion.

Lesson #4: Control over the asset. One important bit of information I want is how much control I have. In the previous chapter on financial IQ #4: leveraging your money, I stated that it was important to invest with control before leverage. If I do not have control, I do not use much leverage. I control my asset value by controlling my rents. My asset value is not based upon a market appraisal, which is an opinion 99 percent of the time.

The reason bankers often ask for a large down payment on a property is simply because they do not trust the appraised value. Of course, this practice went out the window when credit became cheap. With easy credit and cheap money, housing prices skyrocketed as fools rushed in after fool's gold. More buyers meant prices went up. As prices went up, real estate appraisals went up. As appraisals went up, families felt rich because they thought their home went up in value. Many took out home equity loans based upon their new appraised valuations. They bought new cars, vacation homes, took cruises, and went shopping. Then a rip appeared in the balloon, a tiny tear known as a problem with subprime mortgages. As the tiny tear keeps ripping, the balloon starts floating back to earth.

This is the problem with using an opinion (capital gains) rather than a fact (cash flow) as the basis of valuation. This is true not only for real estate, but for all asset classes. This is why when seeking financial information I need to know if the information is a fact or an opinion. Financial insanity is caused when opinions are mistaken for facts.

Fools Rush In

There are two songs worth humming to yourself the next time you are about to make an investment decision, "Fools Rush In" by Johnny Mercer and Rube Bloom, and "The Gambler" by Don Schlitz and sung by Kenny Rogers. The line I love from "The Gambler" is "You never count your money when you're sitting at the table." When someone says, "My net worth is . . . ," or "My home is appraised at . . . ," I know I'm talking to a gambler, a person counting his or her money while sitting at the table. My rich dad said, "The reason you do not count your money while you're sitting at the table is because as long as you are at the table, your money does not belong to you. The moment you step away from the table, the money in your pocket is your money and you can count it."

Today, millions of workers with retirement accounts are counting their money while sitting at the table. Since most investors invest in paper assets and for capital gains, most invest without control and invest upon the hope that *opinions* become *facts*. That is very risky.

This does not mean a smart investor only invests upon the facts. A smart investor is a person who invests with both opinions and facts. A smart investor knows that facts and opinions can be valuable bits of information. Simply said, "A fact is something that is proved by verification of physical proof. An opinion is something that *may or may not* be based upon a fact." In other words, an opinion might be a fact, but it remains an opinion until verified. As my good friend and business partner Ken McElroy says, "Trust, but verify."

Lesson #5: What are the rules? Rules and laws are very important types of information. Many people get into trouble simply because they do not know the rules, ignore the rules, or break the rules.

Personally, I never liked rules. In Vietnam, I liked them even less. One of the things I hated was that we fought according to one set of rules and the enemy fought according to another. One rule I found ridiculous in war was the rule that we could not pursue the enemy across borders. The enemy would fight close to the border and then escape across it for safety. There were many times we had to break off a fight because the VC crossed back into Laos.

Another rule I did not like was that I had to wear a uniform, but the enemy did not. One of the hardest things about fighting was not having the information on who was an enemy and who was not. A uniform would provide that information.

Rules Increase Asset Value

It was my rich dad who changed my attitude towards rules. He said, "If there are no rules, there is no asset." Explaining further he said, "In a neighborhood where the rules are broken, crime is high and property values go down." He also said, "If you play sports and there is no referee to enforce the rules, the game turns into chaos. If you drive on the highway and police do not enforce the rules, people die. This is why rules are important."

Rules can make a person very rich or very poor. This is why information on rules is so important. Not too long ago, the executives of Enron broke the rules; the company disappeared, workers lost their jobs, and investors lost their money. In the world of investing, different assets have different rules. One reason I do not like mutual funds is because I do not like the rules. I have no control. I prefer the rules of real estate, which allow me to make more money and legally pay less in taxes. If I applied the rules of real estate to mutual funds, I would go to jail.

For people who want to be rich, having good accountants and lawyers is important. Today, there are so many laws, rules, and regulations that it is impossible for any one person to know or understand them all. While hiring an attorney or accountant may seem expensive, the pain they can save and money they can make for you can be much greater than the fees you pay them.

Remember two things: Rules provide a valuable source of information about how the game of money is played. And without rules, assets decline in value.

Lesson #6: Trends. A trend is developed when an investor takes information from a set of *facts* and then forms an *opinion*. Let me tell you a story that had a major impact on my life.

In late 1972, the North Vietnamese Army (NVA) crossed the Demilitarized Zone (DMZ). The NVA was on its way to take Saigon, known today as Ho Chi Minh City. The first major city south of the DMZ was Quang Tri. We knew that if we did not stop them there, the war was lost.

As we began to lose the battle for Quang Tri, I noticed some different message traffic. One bit of information was that the South Vietnamese people were trading their currency, the Vietnamese piaster, for gold leaf. I thought this piece of obscure information was interesting.

As stated throughout this book, the U.S. dollar stopped being money and became a currency in 1971. In 1973, while in Vietnam, I directly observed the change in the rules of money via the information received about the panic in the South Vietnamese people's lives. They knew the war was lost and they were on the losing side.

In 1971, gold was pegged at $35 an ounce. In 1973, I watched its price go up past $80 an ounce. As the North Vietnamese began their march south, fear was approaching a panic level. The rich who sided with the U.S. were getting ready to run. Instead of clinging to the piaster or U.S. dollars, they were buying all the gold they could get their hands on. One intelligence report I received stated, "Confidence lost. People ready to flee. Trading dollars and 'P's' [piasters] for gold."

Sitting in the Top Secret room, I realized that people wanted gold. I assumed they knew gold would buy them passage to another country. I could feel their anguish. They knew that gold could save their lives.

I knew the facts. The U.S. was losing the war. The enemy was taking ground. Internationally, the dollar was dropping and gold was going up in price. From the intelligence report, I knew the South Vietnamese people were panicking and dumping their currency to buy gold. To me, this trend was an investment opportunity. I used it to form an opinion.

A few days later a friend and I flew north, just behind enemy lines, hoping to buy some gold. Our *opinion* was the Vietnamese gold miners would be desperate to sell to us their gold since the NVA had just overrun their village. Our *opinion* was the miners would jump at the opportunity to take our U.S. dollars. Our *opinion* was we would be in a good position to buy gold at a discount. Because of our opinion, based upon a few facts, we were willing to break a few rules and risk our lives just to make a few dollars.

Instead of making a killing, I was nearly killed. Instead of buying gold at a discount, I learned a valuable lesson about gold and currencies. That day I found out that the price of gold *really* was the same price all over the world. On that day, the price was about $82 an ounce. I found out that regardless of whether I was buying gold in U.S. territory or NVA territory, its price was the same.

Standing behind enemy lines, hoping to buy gold at a lower price, is a perfect example of becoming smart by being stupid. I was getting an MBA in international finance by standing in front of the bamboo-hut sales office for the mine, arguing with a red-toothed old woman, stained from chewing betel nuts. Although I did not ask, I sincerely doubt if this woman was a Harvard graduate. I doubt if she had any formal education at all, but she was a great teacher. Even though she did not seem to be well-educated, or dressed for success, she knew her stuff when it came to the value and price of gold.

She was financially intelligent and tough as nails. She was not going to let a couple of young American pilots sweet-talk her out of her gold with rapidly declining U.S. dollars.

To this day, I vividly remember standing in front of her, arguing for a $5 discount. I was willing to pay $77, not the world price of $82. Instead of taking our money, she just kept shaking her head and chewing on her betel nuts. She knew the price. She knew the local and geopolitical economic forces in the world. She was informed, she was tuned in, she was cool, and she was in no hurry to sell her gold. She knew the trend was on her side and not on ours, and that there were people far more desperate for her gold than two pilots trying to make a few bucks.

Once it dawned on me that she was not going to budge, I said silently to myself, "I'm dead. Today I am going to die, standing behind enemy lines, asking for a $5 discount. No one will find us. No one will ever know what happened to us. We will be missing in action and we aren't even *in* any action. I won't be killed for a noble cause. I'll be killed trying to shave a few dollars off the price of an international commodity. I will die because I am cheap and stupid. If I stand here any longer, I will be shot in the back, arguing with this woman for a discount. I'm so stupid that I deserve to die."

The Trend Is Your Friend

There were three lessons I learned that day. One was the power of global markets. A global market means the price is the same all over the world. Gold is priced in international markets. Real estate is priced in a local market. The old woman won because she had information from both the global and the local markets. She won because she had better information and higher intelligence.

Today, I understand that I need to know what information

is important both locally and globally. Today, I love real estate because it is an asset more dependent on local information than on global information. With real estate, I can be the expert in my small area. With local information, I can be smarter than the big institutional investors in New York, London, Hong Kong, or Tokyo. Just as David beat Goliath, a small investor with superior information and intelligence can beat the giant.

The second lesson I learned that day was the power of trends. If I had better understood trends and the price of gold, I would have made a lot of money without risking my life behind enemy lines. I did not need to go behind enemy lines to invest. I did not need to ask for a discount. All I had to do was invest with the trend. I could have gone to a coin shop in any town in the world and bought gold for the same price. By 1979, the trend had carried gold to nearly $800 an ounce. I did not have to risk my life. If I had trusted the trend, I would have made a lot of money. I did not need a discount to make money.

The third and most valuable lesson that day was that information is just information. *Intelligence is the ability to take information and make it meaningful.* The old woman with red teeth had the same information I had. Yet her intelligence provided her understanding and meaning I did not have. She was a seasoned player. She knew the game. I was the new kid, a new player in an ancient game.

When the markets crashed and people panicked on August 9, 2007, I thought of that old woman. The first thing I did was check the trends. Instead of joining the crowd and going into panic mode, I simply kept my fear in check, and refocused on the trends in the market, not on its ups or downs. I reverified the facts and formed my own opinion about the future.

I was looking for information on the actions taken by the central banks. Once again they were printing more funny money rather than solving the problem. When I learned the facts, that international central banks were injecting cash into the crashing markets, I knew my opinion that the purchasing power of the dollar would continue to *trend down* was still sound.

Today, instead of diversifying, I prefer to focus on a few small assets, notice a trend, and invest with the trend. Since I know a trend can reverse and change direction, *I do not blindly invest for the long term.* The Information Age is about change and I need to be flexible . . . not a robot.

Some of the trends I am investing in today are:

Trends in oil. As you know, the more China, India, and Eastern Europe become Westernized, the more the demand for oil goes up. Even with the rush to find alternative sources of power, oil will continue to be a primary source of power for years to come. As much as I do not like the environmental damage oil causes, the harsh reality is we all use it, even the most devoted environmentalists. I believe the long-term trend for the price of oil is up, possibly as high as $200 a barrel in the near future. This high price will have serious repercussions upon the world economy, which will later lead to other trends worth following as alternative energy technology, such as solar power, makes advances.

Trends in silver. I believe silver is the best investment in 2007. I believe it is a better investment than oil. There are two reasons I say this. The first reason is because silver is consumable industrial metal. This means it's used up. Silver is the metal of choice for electronics. It is used in computers, cell phones, television sets, and other gadgets. It is estimated that 95 percent of all silver is already consumed. It is becoming scarcer. Gold is different. It is estimated that 95 percent of all gold ever found is still around. Instead of being consumed as silver is, gold is hoarded. In many ways, this makes silver more valuable than gold.

The second reason is because silver is also a precious metal, a form of money. As the dollar drops in purchasing power, more people will look for anything that represents real money or at least holds its value. As I write, silver is very cheap when compared to gold. It is approximately $13 an ounce while gold is approximately $600 an ounce. Historically, gold has been only 14 times the price of silver, which means if silver were $10 an ounce, gold would be trading at $140 an ounce. At today's prices gold and silver are trading at a differential of 50. To me, based on historical trends and the fact that silver is a consumable metal, it has a greater opportunity to go up in price.

About a year ago, many stock exchanges made silver exchange-traded funds (ETFs) available for the investor who did not want to hoard silver coins and bars or invest in silver mining stock. The silver ETF made it easier for investors to invest in silver. A silver ETF is like the old U.S. money, a piece of paper backed by silver, known as a *silver certificate*. The difference is an ETF can go up and down with the fluctuations in the world price of silver. I believe the addition of the silver ETF means the world is getting ready to start hoarding more and more silver as the purchasing power of world currencies continues to go down.

That silver is a consumable and precious metal makes it the investment opportunity of the decade. The reports are that there is less than 300 million ounces of silver left on earth. This means that the world may run out of it by the year 2020. Because of this, a few silver bugs feel that silver will become as expensive as gold in a few years. I do not think it will go that high. Yet, due to the supply-and-demand trends, I believe silver is a once-in-a-lifetime opportunity. Today it's a cheap, low-risk investment anyone in the Western world can afford. That is why I watch the trends and purchase silver anytime the silver market drops in price. Of course I could be wrong, so it is best to do your own research and find your own information before investing in this trend.

Trends in housing. One of the reasons for the high price of commodities is that the world needs and wants more housing. For example, demand for concrete in China caused a shortage of concrete in the U.S., which caused the price of concrete to skyrocket.

One of the reasons I love investing in apartment houses is that, rich or poor, people will pay for a roof over their head. In America, the population is expected to grow from 300 million to over 400 million in the next two decades. So I believe the price of housing will continue to trend up.

As real estate becomes more expensive and difficult to afford, and as wages come down, I believe these trends will cause more people to be renters. One of the reasons Kim and I did not panic during the August 9, 2007, crash is because we *rent out* real estate for cash flow. We do not *sell* real estate. People who invest for *capital gains* are people who buy to *sell* real estate.

When the subprime mortgage market collapsed, sellers panicked. People who invested for cash flow, those who rent property to others, didn't panic. In fact, they saw opportunity. In down markets, there are more renters than buyers, so a crash is generally good for landlords but not sellers.

The old woman chewing on betel nuts and selling gold knew that panic was going to make her rich. The trend was her friend. People who rent their property know that the trend is their friend. For those who sell property, or are counting on their property to appreciate in value, the short-term trends may work against them. Instead of prices' going up, they will probably come down or remain flat. The boom is over for sellers and just beginning for landlords.

Demography Is Destiny

A very valuable source of information is demographics. As the saying goes, "Demography is destiny." In other words, just watch people, as I did in Vietnam, and you'll know which way to invest. Once I knew that when people panic they buy commodities with their currency, I had very valuable information for basing my opinions on trends. As gold went below $400 an ounce, I started to buy a little and began buying a lot when it hit $275 an ounce. Then the price began to head back up. In other words, I followed the trend down and bought a lot once the trend reversed. One of the reasons I like gold and silver is because there is always a market for it. It is relatively liquid, and if I need cash, I can get cash pretty quickly.

Less Liquidity, More Information

In real estate, the trend is a large percentage of baby boomers' retiring to Arizona and Nevada. So I invest in those states. Due to the loss of jobs in Detroit, people are moving out of Detroit, which is pushing housing prices and rents down. It will be a number of years before that trend changes. Since real estate is much less liquid than gold, silver, and stocks, I need to be much more cognizant of trends.

After August 9, 2007, many homeowners, flippers, and real estate developers with overpriced condos are finding it hard to become liquid again. Instead of selling to get out, all most can do is watch helplessly as the value of their real estate sinks into the sunset. The lesson is: the less liquid an investment, the more trend information you need. Many people bought high and now are faced with selling low. An astute investor knows how to follow trends in order to buy low and sell high.

The Financial Bird of Prey

Every time I see developers' construction cranes sitting on high-rise condos I know the end of the trend is near. Whenever you see construction cranes, a.k.a. birds of prey, sitting on the skyline, you know the boom is about to bust. It means that the cycle has peaked, and, generally, there is nowhere to go but down. The next time you see more than two construction cranes on the skyline, start selling any piece of real estate you do not want.

History and Cycles

A final thought on trends is the importance of history and cycles. Having survived a number of up and down markets, I have learned a lot from history. There is one historical financial trend I believe is worth watching. That trend is the twenty-year cycle between stocks and commodities. As a person who sailed for an oil company and flew helicopters in search of gold, I became curious about why the prices of commodities went up as stock prices came down. A few years ago, I came across a book written by one of my favorite financial authors, Jim Rogers, entitled *Hot Commodities.* Rogers discovered that stock prices went up for twenty years at the same time as commodity prices came down.

For example, from 1960 to 1980, just as I was coming of age, commodity prices such as oil and gold were rising. In 1980, oil, gold, silver, and real estate prices came down rapidly as stock prices started climbing. Between 1980 and 2000, the stock market was the place to be, and oil, gold, and silver were dogs. While the commodity market was down, I was buying all the oil, gold, silver, and real estate I could. On schedule, in 2000, at the height of the dotcom boom, share prices dropped and commodity prices came roaring back up. If history repeats, this means that commodities will come down in 2020 and stocks will be the market to be in again.

Obviously, I do not have a crystal ball. But history does seem to repeat, and I am old enough to have seen some reruns. If you would like more information on how a world-class investor such as Jim Rogers analyzes trends, I recommend you read *Hot Commodities*, or any other book he has written. He is a brilliant investor and writer who is an astute observer of trends. Always remember, "The trend is your friend." If you ignore the trend, the birds of prey will pick your bones clean.

In Conclusion

Ultimately, it is not the asset that makes you rich. Information makes you rich . . . or poor. For example, if I had bought gold at $800 an ounce in 1979, I would still be waiting to make my money back today. Given how much the dollar has dropped in purchasing power, that means I would have to wait till gold reached $1,500 to break even today.

The same is true for any asset. For example, in real estate most investors lose money because of inadequate information and intelligence. That is why when someone asks me, "Is real estate a good investment?" my reply is, "I don't know. Are you a good investor?"

Most businesses fail because of a lack of good business information and intelligence rather than from a lack of money. When people ask me, "I have a great idea for a new business, and I'm looking for some money, would you be interested in investing in my new company?" my reply is, "I don't know. How many successful businesses have you started?"

As it turned out, volunteering to fight in Vietnam was one of the smartest things I ever did. If I had not volunteered, I would never have met that old woman chewing betel nuts. That day, standing behind enemy lines, she taught me a very important lesson. She won because she knew the *price of gold* had nothing to do with the *value of gold*. By understanding value, she knew why people were buying and why gold was important to them. That day I learned that it is not the asset that makes you rich . . . it is information and intelligence that makes you rich. If I can lose money investing in gold, which is real money, I can lose money in anything. That day I vowed to become smarter because she taught me that it is information and intelligence that makes me rich . . . not the gold.

Chapter 8

The Integrity of Money

"Integrity" is an interesting word. I have heard it used in many different ways and in different contexts. I believe it is one of the more misused, confused, and abused words in the English language. Many times I have heard someone say, "He has no integrity," or "If they had any integrity, they would be more successful." Someone else might say, "That house has integrity of design." Before discussing the integrity of money, I think it best I give my definition of "integrity."

Webster's offers three definitions for "integrity." They are:

1. *Soundness*: An unimpaired condition.
2. *Incorruptibility*: Firm adherence to a code of especially moral or artistic values.
3. *Completeness*: The quality or state of being complete or undivided.

The Integrity of a Car

All three definitions are required to discuss money and integrity. To better illustrate, I use the example of the integrity of an automobile. An automobile is made up of systems: the brake system, fuel system, electrical system, hydraulic system, and so on. If the systems are not operating in integrity, the car will not function, it will not be *sound*. For example, if the fuel system is *corrupted*, the entire car stops. The integrity of the car is compromised and broken. The car is not *whole*.

The Integrity of Health and Wealth

A similar example can be made with the human body. Some of the systems of the body are the arterial system, respiratory system, nervous system, skeletal system, digestive system, and so on. If the integrity of the human body's system is not sound, corrupted with clogged arteries for instance, health declines and disease or death soon follows.

Just as *health* can break down from a literal lack of integrity, so can *wealth* be compromised by a lack of integrity. Instead of disease or death, which comes from a breakdown in the body's integrity, symptoms of a lack of financial integrity are low income, crippling taxes, high expenses, excessive debt, bankruptcy, foreclosure, increased crime, violence, sadness, and despair.

Earlier, I listed five different financial intelligences. Once again they are:

Financial IQ #1: Making more money.
Financial IQ #2: Protecting your money.
Financial IQ #3: Budgeting your money.
Financial IQ #4: Leveraging your money.
Financial IQ #5: Improving your financial information.

The integrity of all five intelligences is required if a person wants to grow rich, stay rich, and pass his or her wealth on for generations. Missing one or more of the financial intelligences is like someone who doesn't know how to drive attempting to drive a car that has brakes without pads, and water in the gas line.

When a person is struggling financially, one or more of these financial intelligences is out of whack, financial integrity is not sound, and the person is not complete. For example, I have a friend who earns a lot of money as a manager of a small business. Her problem is she has no protection against taxes, plus she does not budget well, spends impulsively to buy clothes and take vacations. Her leverage is a big home because she thinks real estate only goes up in price. She gets her financial advice from her husband and his financial planner. Her husband is a great guy but, like his wife, he has similar challenges with all five financial intelligences.

They are nice people, educated, honest, churchgoing, and hardworking. They enjoy life and raise great kids. The problem is a lack of financial integrity. This lack of financial integrity shows up as worry about borrowing the equity out of their home to pay off credit card bills, affording a college education for their three kids, and having enough for retirement. These are typical money problems, symptoms of a lack of financial integrity.

The problem is they don't think they have a problem. They get up every day, send the kids off to school, and go to work. They come home, play with the kids, help them with their homework, watch a little TV, and go to bed. They know something is wrong, but they'd rather not find out what. They're hoping something will change.

Financial Report Card

Like most people, my friends don't have personal financial statements. They don't even know what financial statements are or why they are important. Like most college graduates, my friends left school not knowing the difference between a credit application, a credit score, and a financial statement.

Without a personal financial statement, however, they do not know where they are financially, what might be wrong, and where they might be out of financial integrity. Without a financial statement and the five financial intelligences, it may be difficult to determine what is wrong and what needs to be corrected.

In my opinion, this is where the *lack of integrity* begins. It begins in our school system—with financial IQ #5: improving your financial information. In 1974, when businesses began requiring employees to invest for their retirement, the school system should have added or improved financial education in the curriculum. This lack of financial education in our schools is sending shock waves through the financial integrity of the world.

A Reflection of Financial Integrity

As my rich dad said, "My banker has never asked me for my report card." The reason bankers don't ask for an academic report card is because they are looking for financial intelligence, not academic intelligence. This is why they ask for a financial statement. A financial statement is a reflection of your financial integrity. It is the equivalent of your financial report card.

Bankers are looking for answers that relate to the five financial intelligences. Obviously, they want to know how smart people are at making money, protecting their money, budgeting their money, leveraging their money, and how informed they are. A financial statement will give the bank the information it is looking for.

Out of Financial Integrity

If a person is out of *financial integrity*—as shown by excessive debt, not budgeting well, spending more than he or she earns, foreclosures, and bankruptcies—the banker will probably not want this person as a client. It is a matter of *professional integrity.*

In 2007, with the crash of the credit markets, it became obvious that the credit, banking, and investment institutions have been out of financial integrity. Greed replaced sound lending practices. The economy cannot expand on credit alone. By failing to teach much about money and to expand financial intelligence in school, the system creates adults who are unprepared for our brave new world. Billions of adults across the planet do not have a personal financial statement, cannot read a business's financial statement, and do not know the financial condition of their country. This is a breakdown in educational integrity.

Intrinsic Value

Warren Buffett does not diversify. Instead he looks for a company with *intrinsic value*, a company with financial integrity. He wants to know if the business has the five financial intelligences. In overly simplified terms, Buffett wants the answers to the following questions:

1. Can the business make more money?
2. Does the business have a protected niche?
3. Does the business budget its money and resources well?
4. Can the business be leveraged and expanded?
5. Is it run by a team of smart, well-informed people?

In even simpler terms, intrinsic value means:

1. Niche. This means the business has a core competence, something that will make money in good times and bad. Coca-Cola fits this requirement. People will always drink sugared water regardless if plain water is better for them.

A big advantage Coca-Cola has is its trademark, which is

protected by law. You may recall that financial intelligence #2 is protection. In this case, Warren likes this product because it's a product that is a legally protected brand, not just a commodity. A well-recognized brand, protected and defended from pirates, increases Coca-Cola's intrinsic value.

The brand Rich Dad is a trademark protected by law in every country we do business in. Being a brand gives my business greater intrinsic value. Many authors write books but fail to build a brand. As you know, Harry Potter is a megabrand. So is Donald Trump. If you are not a brand, you are a commodity. Brands have more intrinsic value, and to maintain this value, a brand must be true to its message and customers.

A few years ago, a large mutual fund company approached me and asked if I would endorse its fund. Although the fee it would have paid me was very high, I turned the offer down. In my mind, endorsing a mutual fund would not be true to the Rich Dad brand. To me, it would have shown a lack of integrity, which would diminish the brand's intrinsic value. Besides, I couldn't do it with a straight face.

2. Leverage. This point separates the small business owners from the big business owners. For example, if I am a doctor, it is hard for me to leverage my value if my patients come only to see me. But if that same doctor invented a new cure or kind of medicine, then that doctor's medical intelligence can be *leveraged* via a product.

The world is filled with small business owners and professionals who are not able to leverage because they are the product. Most employees fall into this category. They don't know how to leverage their services and trade time for dollars.

Most of us know musicians who work hard but do not earn much money simply because they fail to leverage their talents. The world is filled with musicians who produce a

CD, which is a form of leverage, but are not able to leverage the distribution and sale of their CD. This is why amateur programs such as *American Idol* are so popular. People who think they can sing want the leverage of national television, even if Simon criticizes them.

3. Expandability. Once a product or business can be leveraged, the next question Warren wants to know is, "How far can the leverage be expanded?" Warren loves Coca-Cola because its leverage is *expandable* throughout the world. Warren says, "Every time someone in the world drinks a Coke, I make a little money."

When I wrote *Rich Dad Poor Dad*, the book was my leverage. Instead of my teaching in person, my book and my games could now do the teaching. The next task was to expand the product into different countries by printing the books and games in different languages. This was done by *licensing* the rights to produce Rich Dad products to businesses in different parts of the world. Instead of having my company print, inventory, and distribute my products, there are now publishers in 109 countries that do that for me. This is my example of *leverage* and then *expandability*.

4. Predictability. What Warren Buffett wants to know is how predictable revenue is. He doesn't want peaks and valleys in income. He wants to know that come rain or shine, the money will come in like clockwork.

One of the reasons I love my apartment houses is that rain or shine, the money comes in. I am not worried about the price of real estate going up or coming down. I want my money coming in 24/7 from all over the world and from my apartment houses.

This is why Warren Buffett does not *diversify*. Instead he focuses on a business's *intrinsic value*. Recognizing intrinsic value requires the five financial intelligences. When a business has intrinsic value, the business has integrity. When a business has integrity, it has a better chance to grow and remain profitable, regardless of changing economic conditions.

Before investing in a company, a professional investor looks at the business's financial statement. The professional investor is looking for business integrity. The same is true when a real estate investor buys an apartment house. Knowing about the internal rate of return (IRR) is intrinsic value applied to real estate.

The problem for most people, due to a lack of financial education in school and not being able to read a financial statement, is that they don't know if the company or real estate they are investing in has financial integrity and intrinsic value.

The Language of Business

Warren Buffett says, "Accounting is the language of business." If you do not know the language, it's hard to tell if the business has integrity. The reason the Rich Dad Company produces our *CASHFLOW* games for adults and children is because we strongly believe that financial intelligence and being able to speak the language of business are crucial in a world of greed and questionable integrity.

Government Financial Integrity

Governments also require the five financial intelligences. Governments need to make money, protect their money, budget their money, leverage their money, and seek the best financial information. If a government operates in integrity, the government and its people flourish. If a government is out of integrity, the government and its people struggle and grow poorer. Higher taxes and excessive debt are signs that the U.S. government is struggling with financial integrity.

In 1971, when Nixon took the U.S. off the gold standard and got the world to accept our currency as the reserve currency of the world, the U.S. went out of financial integrity. Today, rather than being the richest country in the world, we are the biggest debtor nation in the world. While many people have become very rich because of this change in the rules of money, me included, millions more have fallen behind financially. The financial gap is growing wider and becoming dangerous.

The problem for America began at financial intelligence #3: budgeting your money. When America began to import more than it exported, we changed the rules of money and began accumulating trillions of dollars of debt instead of solving the problem, which would have been the intelligent thing to do.

When looking at financial intelligence #4, it becomes apparent the U.S. government doesn't leverage money . . . instead it leverages debt. Today, the richest people in the world are in debt to the poorest people in the world. Talk about being out of integrity.

The U.S. went out of financial integrity when it asked the world to accept a dollar "backed by the full faith and credit" of the U.S. government. No one likes investing in the U.S. and seeing the value of the dollar drop. When the world demands the money back, it will be financial intelligence #2, protection from predators, that will be tested. I believe that the U.S. will become a giant predator, possibly defaulting on some of its loans and its promises to senior citizens for health care and Social Security. It will allow inflation to destroy workers' earnings and raise taxes on the young. To me, this is out of integrity.

The current way for the U.S. government to increase financial intelligence #1: making more money, is by raising taxes, printing more money, borrowing more money, fighting a new war, and not paying a few bills. Obviously, this will cause many more financial problems, which could have been avoided if the earlier problems had been solved in the first place.

The Age of Integrity

History does repeat. Our leaders and educators have been aware of what happens when governments violate the integrity of money. This has happened before. Copernicus in 1517 wrote that inflation was one of the "scourges that debilitate kingdoms." In 1776, Adam Smith said inflation causes "the most pernicious subversion of the fortunes of private people." Smith's warning came true more recently in Germany, when Hitler rose to power, after the Weimar government subverted the integrity of its currency.

The only reason the U.S. and world public isn't finding out about the difference between money and currency is because our school systems simply are out of educational integrity, failing to produce a financially literate populace.

Personally, I believe we as a people, a nation, and the world are all heading for a perfect storm. After being out of integrity for so long, I believe the financial, political, environmental, and spiritual forces will demand that the pendulum swing in the other direction. Exactly what will happen, I do not know. It may have already started.

Unfortunately, the super-rich—those who benefit the most from the current system—will be least affected by the coming financial upheavals. It is the rest of us that will feel the forces of nature and be required to do our best to battle the storm, and the poor will suffer the most.

The good news is that the problems ahead will make us smarter if we take them on with courage, and do not run from them. Inside every problem is a gem of wisdom, a gem that makes us smarter, stronger, and able to do better regardless of economic conditions.

Even more good news is that a few national governments

are beginning to implement financial education courses into their educational systems. I predict that the country that has the best financial education will lead the world into a new era of economic prosperity. After all, this is the Information Age.

Increase Your Intrinsic Value

In the meantime, it is important for each of us to prepare for the potential storm ahead.

My recommendations are:

1. *Put your house in order.* Just like a sailor preparing his boat for a storm, start making your financial boat more sea-worthy. Take a look at the five intelligences and ask yourself which intelligence you need to work on now. Which one needs the most work? Which one is your biggest problem? Focus on that one and address it now. Do not attempt to take all five on at once. That would be overwhelming. I believe you will find that all five are related, so by focusing on one, you will ultimately improve all five intelligences. Then take your time, learning a little every day. Always remember, no golfer became a professional in one day. Not even Tiger Woods.

By increasing your five financial intelligences you are increasing your financial integrity and your own intrinsic value. If you are not sure what to do, please do not be afraid or ashamed to ask for help. In the next chapter on finding your financial genius, I write about how much I depend upon smart people for help. No one is above needing help.

2. *Invest in assets with intrinsic value.* Take another look at some of the criteria Warren Buffett uses to establish a business's intrinsic value. Then for practice, start asking yourself which businesses around you meet the requirements. Even if you do not invest, this is a great exercise for increasing your financial IQ.

Intrinsic Value of Real Estate

One of the reasons I like real estate is because I am able to see, touch, and control much of the property's intrinsic value. But always remember, most real estate is not a good investment. A great exercise, regardless if you have money, is to look at a number of properties and analyze their intrinsic value.

One of the beauties of real estate is creativity. For example, I can use creative financing, creative improvements, or creative ways to increase the value of the property. Creativity is not as much an advantage when picking a stock or buying mutual funds. But in real estate, creativity plus integrity can make you very rich.

3. Batten down the hatches. As they taught us at the U.S. Merchant Marine Academy, when a storm approaches, it is time to *batten down the hatches*. This means to protect the integrity of the ship. In my few years of going to sea, I had the opportunity to sail through four typhoons in the Pacific. Today, I can still see monstrous waves, a mountain of water, crashing over the entire ship. I can see, feel, and hear the ship creaking and straining, doing its best to maintain structural integrity and come out from under the wave. I am glad the engineers designed a great ship, and that the ship's crew was trained and ready to take on the storms.

Chaos is going to increase as the Industrial Age ends and the Information Age takes control. As oil goes up in price, the dollar drops, China and India start producing cars and planes, manufacturing jobs disappear, corporations move offshore, baby boomers expect to be taken care of by the government, terrorism increases, wars we cannot afford are fought, and debt that has to be repaid is increased, problems previously swept under the rug will be exposed. In the Information Age, information such as the five financial intelligences will be your greatest of assets.

I believe the financial integrity of the world is going to be challenged as never before in history. I believe this because there has been too much greed, misinformation, and corruption running our businesses, governments, and schools. In August of 2007, when the credit markets crashed, I believe we were touching the ragged outer limits of the brewing storm. The eye of the storm is still a few years away. Take this time to prepare for the ride of your life. Be brave and get smart because it's going to get exciting. It's going to be a great time to become even richer and become even smarter. But you've got to be brave, and you've got to develop your financial genius.

Chapter 9

Developing Your Financial Genius

I didn't know I wasn't smart until I went to school. For seventeen years, from kindergarten all the way through college, school was a struggle. I was always labeled an *average* student. No matter which class I was in, there were always kids who were smarter, more gifted, and faster learners than me. School seemed easy for the smart kids. School was tough for me. The only A I ever received was in woodshop because I loved working with my hands. I built a boat for my class project while my classmates were making salad bowls for their moms.

I also didn't know I was *poor* until I went to school. When I was nine years old, my family moved across town, and I went to a school for rich kids. Interestingly, there were two elementary schools directly across the street from each other. On one side of the street was Union School. On the other side was Riverside School. Both were public schools, one school for the rich and the other for the working class.

Originally, Union School was for the children of the sugar plantation union workers, hence the school's name. Riverside was the school for the children of sugar plantation owners and managers. I attended Riverside School because the house our family lived in happened to be on the side of the street next to the river.

Even though I was only nine, I was aware that my classmates at Riverside School lived at a higher standard of living than my family. Many of my rich classmates lived in an isolated community connected by a bridge across the river. Every time I crossed that bridge to play with my friends, I knew I was crossing into a different world.

On their side of the bridge, my classmates lived in stately plantation manor homes. On my side of the bridge, homes were a lot less stately. The home we lived in was a home built for plantation workers. My classmates' parents owned their homes. My parents rented. Some of my classmates even had more than one home, many having beach houses. When my family went to the beach, we went to a public beach park. My classmates *played* at the yacht club or the country club. I *worked* at the country club.

Although rich, my classmates and their families were not snobs. They were friendly people involved in the community. I spent a lot of time at my friends' beach homes, on their boats, and flying in their planes. They did not flaunt their wealth. They shared it. To them, being rich seemed natural, not special. It was a lifestyle and a standard of living. Their lifestyle was not that big a deal to them. It was I who thought their lifestyle was a big deal, sometimes feeling uncomfortable, sometimes out of place, and acutely aware of the standard of living that separated us. At the age of twelve, my rich friends went off to private schools, and I continued on through public high school with the kids who went to Union School.

I also didn't know I was a geek until I went to school. In high school, all the girls I wanted to date wanted nothing to do with me. I was not cool. The popular girls were interested in the bad boys who were older, belonged to a gang, and owned a car. Although I was a starting player on the football team and a surfer, I was not cool, not a bad boy, and didn't own a car. I was shy, fat, and drove around in our family's beige-colored station wagon. Definitely not cool.

In 1974, as I was getting out of the Marine Corps at the age of twenty-seven, I knew I wanted to be rich, drive fast cars, and date beautiful women. Even though I had grown up, lost my baby fat, and gotten taller and stronger, in my mind I was still the shy fat guy without much money. I knew what I wanted. I just didn't know how I was going to get there.

I knew I wanted to be an entrepreneur and invest in real estate, but I had no money and no skills. The more I thought about it and compared the life I wanted with what I had, the more I realized that my schoolteachers were correct. I was average. I had no great skills or talent. I was not smart. If I was going to be rich, I needed to find a way to be at least *above* my means in every way.

Don't Live below Your Means

Financial experts advise people to *live below their means* and *diversify*. To many people this sounds like smart advice. The problem with following this advice is that you wind up *average* because it is *average* advice. It is not bad advice. It's just average financial advice. Besides, who wants to live below their means?

In high school, students begin focusing on their academic strengths and taking courses with an eye towards high-paying future careers. Kids are constantly pushed to be smart, study hard, and get good grades. After graduating from college, many go on to graduate school, narrowing career choices to becoming lawyers, doctors, accountants, and MBAs. Many doctors, after years of grueling medical school, go on for additional training to become specialists such as surgeons or internists. Artistic students become artists in clay, oils, watercolors, commercial graphics, and music. Gifted student-athletes prepare for professional careers in football, tennis, basketball, or golf. In fact, if you go to athletic events, many parents scream for blood, demanding their kids play and their team wins. Nobody wants to play on an average team.

Most of us know that to be successful in school and to have successful careers we need to do our best to be the best. We need to focus and study. We need to specialize. Yet when it comes to money, people are advised to *diversify* instead of *specialize* and *live below their means* rather than *live at a higher standard of living.*

When I got out of the Marine Corps I did not want to get an average job and live below my means. To me, *living below your means* is how *below-average people live.* I did not want to drive an average car or live in an average neighborhood. I also knew that *diversifying* would cause my return on investment to be below average. I knew I needed to *focus* if I wanted *a higher standard of living . . .* a standard of living like my classmates who lived across the bridge.

When I looked at the world I was about to reenter after four years of military school and five years in the Marines, I noticed that most people worked hard to be *above average professionally* but were *below average financially.*

I decided the best way to beat the A students, the rich kids, the teachers who labeled me average, and the girls who were not interested in me was to become rich. I was not angry with them. I was just tired of being average. I realized I could become richer than most people because when it came to money, most people were following *below-average* financial strategies and advice.

Why Do Experts Recommend Diversification?

As Warren Buffett says, "Diversification is a protection against ignorance. [It] makes very little sense for those who know what they are doing." Buffett also said about money managers, "Full-time professionals in other fields, let's say dentists, bring a lot to the layman. But in aggregate, *people get nothing for their money from professional money managers.*"

I believe that when many recommend diversification, it is simply a protection against their ignorance. I suspect Buffett is saying that it's below-average financial advice from below-average advisors for below-average investors.

Warren Buffett has a different financial strategy. He doesn't diversify. He focuses. He looks for a great business at a great price. He doesn't buy a lot of businesses and pray one of them does well. He doesn't want average returns, or to play the stock market. He likes to control the company, but not run the company. When Warren talks about investing, his key words are *intrinsic value*, not *diversification*.

One reason financial advisors recommend diversification is that they cannot find great companies. They do not have control, and most don't know how to run a business. They are employees, not entrepreneurs like Warren.

Smart Guys Fail

On August 24, 2007, after the market crash, the *Wall Street Journal* ran a story about how quantitative funds (quants), supposedly managed by some of the smartest guys on Wall Street, all lost money (Justin Lahart, "How the 'Quant' Playbook Failed"). In other words, A students received Fs. The article states:

> Even if they don't share the same statistical models, quant funds share similar approaches to the market.

They are schooled in the same statistical methods, pore over the same academic papers, and use the same historical data. As a result, they can easily come to similar conclusions about how to invest.

In other words, Wall Street hires academic geniuses, A students and graduates of the world's best business schools who use sophisticated computer models to invest billions of dollars, and they all come to the same answer. When their models say "buy" they all buy the same stocks, causing a boom, and when the models say "sell" they sell en masse, crashing the market. This is not financial intelligence.

Not Diversified . . . but Thinking They Are Diversified

I have two very smart classmates who both went on to graduate from Stanford University with PhDs. Both have high-paying jobs, one with a bank and the other with an oil company. After the stock market crashed following 9/11, both lost a lot of money even though both were diversified. Over the years, I talked to them individually. I asked about their investment strategy. Both said, "I invested in a well-diversified portfolio of stocks, bonds, and mutual funds."

Although I did not say it, I wanted to point out to them that they were not really diversified. *Instead of being diversified, they were 100 percent invested in paper assets, primarily the stock market*. They were not in investment-grade real estate, privately held businesses, or commodities such as oil production. When the market went down, it all came down. They were not diversified, but they thought they were. They had above-average academic IQs, but below-average financial IQs.

Finding Your Genius

I built and rebuilt several businesses from 1974 to 1984. I was determined to become an entrepreneur. Just like a baby who stands and falls a number of times before learning to walk, I stood and fell a number of times before walking as an entrepreneur. I did this because I wanted to learn to be an insider, not an outsider.

From 1984 to 1994, I became an educational entrepreneur because I became interested in how people learn. Although I disliked school, I enjoyed learning. Also, I wanted to know why I always felt stupid in class. During those ten years, Kim and I built an education company that taught entrepreneurship and investing from our offices in Australia, Canada, New Zealand, Singapore, and the U.S.

During this period of time I did things differently, almost the opposite of the way traditional schools teach. Instead of creating an environment where only one or two students were smart, I created an environment where everyone could feel smart and learn. Instead of *competing,* the class *cooperated.* Instead of having students listen to me lecture, I created different games to teach specific subjects. Instead of being bored, adult students were actively challenged, and participated.

I went on to develop my educational board game *CASH-FLOW* from what I learned as an entrepreneurial educator, the first game to teach both accounting and investing at the same time. As you may know, accounting can be the most boring subject on earth and investing the most frightening. By combining the two subjects into one game, learning became challenging, and fun. A person could play the game a thousand times and still learn something new about accounting, investing, and themselves. The game was officially launched in 1996.

As I learned more about the human mind and how we

learn, I found out a number of things about our school system that were disturbing. I found out that our current system of teaching actually damages a child's brain. In other words, even an A student can be slowed up by the educational system. The more I studied and practiced different teaching techniques in my classes, the more I began to find the answers I was looking for, and I found why I had constantly been labeled stupid or, at best, average.

Multiple Intelligences

Through my research I discovered the book *Frames of Mind: The Theory of Multiple Intelligences* by Howard Gardner. His work was mind-expanding and validating. He teaches that there are seven intelligences:

1. Linguistic
2. Logical-mathematical
3. Musical
4. Bodily-kinesthetic
5. Spatial
6. Interpersonal
7. Intrapersonal

His book validated what I intrinsically knew; I simply didn't have the intelligences recognized by the school system, which are predominantly linguistic and logical-mathematical. This is one of the reasons I failed English twice in high school. I could not write, spell, or punctuate. I am not *linguistic*, and I am not *logical*.

In my freshman year at the Merchant Marine Academy, English became my favorite subject because I had a great teacher. If not for that teacher, I might not be an author today. My English teacher at the academy had great *interpersonal* skills, which is why he could relate to me. I respected him. Instead of talking down to me, he inspired me. We could speak person to person rather than teacher to student. In his class, I wanted to be smart, and I wanted to learn. Instead of another F in English, I received a B.

I Need Security

Later, as a Marine in Vietnam, it was my *intrapersonal* intelligence that kept me alive. Intrapersonal intelligence is the ability to control your emotions and get the job done, even if the job is life-threatening. Many people are not successful financially because their intrapersonal intelligence is weak. People with limited intrapersonal intelligences often say, "I need job security," or "That sounds risky." These are examples of emotions doing the thinking, not intrapersonal intelligence.

As I studied more about Gardner and his theory of multiple intelligences, I realized that the A students were those who had high linguistic and logical-mathematical intelligences. Reading, writing, and math were easy for them but very difficult for me. I read and wrote slowly, and I only liked math if I was measuring something like my boat or my money. My intelligence strengths were spatial, bodily-kinesthetic, and intrapersonal, which is why I doodled in class, built a boat, and was not threatened or motivated when teachers told me I wouldn't get a good job if I didn't get good grades.

At this time, you may want to ask yourself: of the seven intelligences, which are you strongest at? You may want to list them in order, one being the highest and seven being the lowest. I encourage you to read Dr. Gardner's book.

Three Parts of the Brain

Albert Einstein is credited with saying, "Imagination is more important than knowledge."

As an entrepreneurial educator, I did a lot of research on the different parts of the brain. Boiling it all down to overly simplified terms, we have three basic parts to our brain, pictured below.

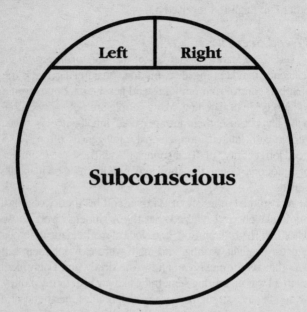

1. *The left brain.* Generally this part of the brain is used for reading, writing, speaking, and logic. Kids who do well in school have well-developed left brains. From Gardner's work on multiple intelligences, the left brain would be most associated with *linguistic*, *logical-mathematical*, and *interpersonal* intelligences. Writer, scientist, lawyer, accountant, and schoolteacher are professions for such people.

2. *The right brain.* This part of the brain is often associated with pictures, art, music, and other more nonlinear relationships—with creativity and imagination. From Gardner's work, *musical* and *spatial* intelligences would be most associated with the right brain. Designer, architect, and musician are professions for people with these dominant intelligences.

3. *The subconscious brain.* This is the most powerful of the three brains because it includes the "old brain," often called the primitive brain. It's the primitive brain that is most like an animal's brain. It does not think, but rather reacts, fights, flees, or freezes. From Gardner's work, the *intrapersonal* intelligence would most relate to the subconscious mind. In my opinion, it is a person's intrapersonal intelligence that ultimately determines if they are a success or failure in life, love, health, and money. This is because the subconscious mind is the most powerful part of the brain, especially in pressure situations.

The subconscious mind also affects our bodily actions via *bodily-kinesthetic* intelligence. For example, in the game of golf, pressure may cause a golfer to choke and miss an easy putt. Subconsciously, a person may freeze and not take action out of fear of making a mistake, or stay at a job for security rather than the love of the work.

People with high intrapersonal intelligence have the ability to control the subconscious brain's desire to fight, flee, or freeze. Instead of *flee*, they may decide the best thing to do is *freeze*. If *frozen*, they may choose to *fight*. The point is, they have the intelligence to choose the appropriate subconscious response. If angry, they can speak calmly. If afraid, they can confront their fear.

People think differently when their subconscious is controlled by fear. If people are fearful they may say, "I can't do that. What if I fail?" or "That's risky." Compare that to a person who is in a fight-state subconsciously, who might say, "I'll show them. I'll get that deal just to prove I can do it."

Learning to choose your subconscious state of mind *before* thinking and making decisions is very important. When I was in Vietnam, I felt better, flew better, and was more confident when I subconsciously chose to fight. When I was in a fleeing or fearful state, my thoughts were fearful. So choose your subconscious state of mind before using your left and right brains.

Professions requiring tremendous control under stress are best for people with strong *intrapersonal* intelligence. For example, police officers, emergency room nurses and doctors, firefighters, and soldiers require high intrapersonal intelligence. I would say entrepreneurs require a high level of this intelligence.

Which Brain Controls Your Money?

The reason I became curious about the brain and how it works is because I wondered why so many people say one thing and then do another. For example, I might ask a person, "Do you want to be rich?" Most people will say from their logical left brain, "Yes. I really want to be rich." The problem is not found in their logical left brain. The problem is the subconscious brain's saying, "Not you. You'll never be rich," or "How can you be rich, you don't have any money."

In most cases, it's the subconscious *fear of failing* that holds people back. It is this fear of failing that teachers use to motivate people in school. I remember my teachers saying to me, "If you don't get good grades, you won't get a good job." Later in life, when the A students who got the good jobs want to make career changes, their fear holds them prisoner.

For example, I have a friend who is an attorney, an A student from Harvard, who wants to change, but he can't. He is afraid of doing something new for fear of failing and not making enough money. He says to me, "I've been an attorney for so long I don't know what else to do. Who else will pay me what I am earning?" He has a brilliant left brain, an underdeveloped right brain, and an out-of-control subconscious brain.

Again, the subconscious brain is the most powerful of the three brains. The subconscious mind is so powerful that it controls our addictions. For example, most smokers want to quit. You can logically explain to their left brain all the harmful effects of smoking and show their right brain horrifying pictures of lung cancer. But if the subconscious mind wants to smoke, the person smokes. In many ways the subconscious brain controls your life, regardless if you are an A or F student. For most people, when it comes to money, there is a *battle of the brains* going on inside of them. It is this conflict that causes many people to *live below their means* when in reality they want to *improve their standard of living* and to be rich.

As a teacher of entrepreneurship and money, I find many people, even well-educated ones, who are addicted to being poor. Something in their brain keeps them poor. Instead of turning everything they touch to gold, everything they touch turns to lead.

Battle of the Brains

As a teacher, this battle of the brains made me curious. I was puzzled by the conflict between a person's logical and illogical mind. I realized that true education isn't simply a matter of teaching students to read, write, and memorize answers. I realized that to be effective true education had to align the power of all three brains. Instead of the three brains' working against each other, they had to work together. If a person could align and develop all three brains, he or she had a greater chance of success in the real world.

The problem with traditional education is that it focuses on only one part of the brain, the left brain. In other words, you could be a left-brain genius and a subconscious moron. You can know what to do in your left brain and in your subconscious brain be terrified of actually doing it. Worst of all, many people leave school, fully able to read, write, and do math, but are terrified of failing and seek security instead of opportunity in the real world. They're taught to value knowledge over imagination—and over the ability to integrate all three parts of the brain. After years of striving to be the best, these people are told by financial experts to *diversify* and *live below their means*. To a fearful subconscious brain, this advice sounds intelligent and logical. For years these people then turned over a portion of their paycheck every month to their financial experts with the hopes that they know what they're doing. At the same time, the richest investor in the world, Warren Buffett, says, "Diversification is a protection against ignorance." And it is.

A World Ruled by Left-Brainers

The world is run by left-brained people. The problem with left-brained people is they think there is only one brain and only one intelligence. Many are not aware of the other parts of the brain and the possibility of other types of intelligences. When you ask a highly educated left-brained person for the definition of intelligence, he or she replies, "If you agree with me you are intelligent. If you don't, you're an idiot."

In the world of money, these left-brained people believe making money is a by-the-numbers formula, a mathematical equation. This is why when the market crashed many funds crashed in unison. The funds are run by academic geniuses all following the same formula. Here's another quote from the August 24, 2007, *Wall Street Journal* article on quant funds (Justin Lahart, "How the 'Quant' Playbook Failed"):

> A number of quant funds, which use statistical models to find winning trading strategies, reported heavy losses this month. In many cases, the managers pointed their fingers at other quantitative hedge funds, essen-

tially saying they all owned many of the same stocks and their models told them to sell at the same time, driving down the share prices, hurting everyone in the process.

In other words, the A students used their linguistic and logical-mathematical left brains to invest in the stock market and came up with the same answers . . . just like in school. And who pays the price for the losses? Not the A students. They have steady paychecks. They are employees, not investors.

Learning to Win Using Your Whole Brain

Warren Buffett once said, "You have to think for yourself. It always amazes me how high-IQ people mindlessly imitate."

As an educational entrepreneur, I began teaching students to think outside the box and to create rather than imitate. I was surprised at how frightening this teaching process was for many of my students. Most had been so frightened into needing job security, a magic formula for investing, and avoiding mistakes that breaking the bonds of that fear was the hardest part of my job. These were smart, successful, well-educated people who wanted to make changes. They were not poor, unsuccessful, and uneducated.

My job as a teacher was to show them how to use their primary intelligences and all three brains to win financially. I often called my business programs "Learning to Win Using Your Whole Brain." To get people's attention, I would often say, "A students work for the C students, and B students work for the government." Obviously this did not make the A students happy, but they got over it once I explained the logic behind my findings.

Poor and Middle-Class Dialects

Neuroscientists have recently discovered that the brain has mirror neurons. Many of these scientists believe this discovery is more important than the discovery of DNA. A neuromirror, in overly simple terms, is the equivalent of *monkey see, monkey do* or *birds of a feather flock together.* That is, our brains are programmed to imitate what we see others do. It explains why quant fund managers invest in the same stocks, why poor people stay poor even though they earn a lot of money, and why a child raised in England will speak a different dialect of English with a different accent than a child born in the U.S. or Australia.

Mirror neurons of dialect and accent limit the scope of our world and who we associate with. Many kids have a tough time leaving Hawaii because their dialect of English is Pidgin English. Kids from Hawaii who speak Pidgin often go to mainland schools with big Hawaiian clubs so they can feel comfortable. Many of the kids at Union School spoke Pidgin. The kids from Riverside School were forbidden to speak it. I believe this made a tremendous difference in my life, and why I went to school in New York and not at the University of Hawaii.

In the world of business and investing, poor people speak a poor person's dialect. Instead of using the language of business and investing, they say such things as, "Government programs, welfare, and assistance." The middle class has a different dialect. They say, "Diversify and live below your means." Buffett, the richest investor in the world, says, "It's not that I want money. It's the fun of making money and watching it grow." Again, this is an example of a different English dialect reflecting a different mirror-neuron brain.

Every group speaks a different dialect. For example, when golfers get together they speak a completely different form of English. When they talk about a *birdie*, they are not talking about shooting wild birds on the golf course. Wherever you go in the world, if one golfer says to another golfer, "I shot a birdie," every golfer knows this person scored one below par, which means it was above-average play.

In the same way, simply put, rich people speak a different dialect. It's a matter of different brains and different mirror neurons. That is why crossing the bridge at age nine was life-changing and why I do not live below my means or diversify. This is why even when I was broke, I did not drive cheap cars, wear cheap clothes, or live in a cheap neighborhood. It's a matter of mirror neurons and of standard of living.

Today, neuroscientists believe that mirror neurons are the most powerful learning parts of our brains. In the classroom, it explains why some students are teacher's pets. Since most classrooms are led by left-brained people, they tend to favor the kids with the same intelligences. On the flip side, these teachers tend not to like kids who are artistic, musical, creative, physical learners, or not easily intimidated. By the time college comes around, most of the kids who are not linguistic and logical-mathematical are gone. They have been labeled and eliminated. Sadly, the kids who are eliminated often leave school feeling stupid. Imagine if that happens to you at an early age. How does this label affect the rest of your life?

In an experiment conducted by Harvard professor Robert Rosenthal and Lenore Jacobson in 1966, teachers were told that certain kids in their classes were geniuses even though they were not. In almost all cases, those kids received exceptionally high grades. In other words, researchers found that it was the teacher's perception of the child's intelligence that had the greatest influence on a child's learning. In the world of investing this is called a *bias*; in race relations it is known as a *prejudice*. This is an example of the impact of mirror neurons.

In simple terms, mirror neurons mean our brains are like television transmitters and receivers. Even though we are not physically talking to one another, our brains are communicating at very deep levels. For example, when we walk into a room, most of us can immediately sense who likes us and who doesn't, even though nothing is said. This is the worst part. I learned that if I did not feel good about myself, people did not feel good about me. In many instances, another person is only sending back what I am broadcasting. In other words, if I think I am a loser, other people will think of me as a loser.

The good news is that you and I can change their perception of us by changing our perceptions of ourselves. This can be done by adapting our mirror neurons. It is not easy, but it can be done. For example, if I had not changed my perception of myself, I would never have met and married a beautiful woman like Kim, someone like Donald Trump wouldn't be my friend, and I wouldn't be financially secure today. If I had not consciously changed my perception, I would probably still be a shy, fat, poor kid speaking Pidgin English.

Even though I graduated from a very good school, I left not feeling smart. I left feeling that there were people I would never be as smart as. I was always average. When I interviewed for jobs, the first questions asked were what school I went to and if I had a master's degree. If I had a master's degree I had a better chance of being hired. Once again, even though I was in the business world, I was still in a classroom, in a world dominated by left-brain intelligence. In 1974, while working at Xerox, promising the company that I would get my MBA, I began researching the brain and different ways of learning and teaching. I was looking for a way to win on my terms, not on their terms.

Being raised in a family of schoolteachers, I realized their measure of success was the school a person attended and how many advanced degrees he or she had. In the world of big business, it was pretty much the same thing. In most major corporations, employers want the pedigree of prestige that comes with advanced degrees from recognized schools. In other words, graduates from Ivy League schools are better than graduates of state universities, who are better than graduates of community colleges. In the world of big business, the school you attended can give you a better job, a better title, and a better paycheck. That is the measure of success.

Being around my rich dad, I realized his measure of success was how much money he made, the people he spent time with, the freedom to work or not work, and how many jobs he provided. I realized I had better decide whose measure of success I wanted to base my life on. Since I did not think I could win at my poor dad's game of school and big business, I decided I had a better chance of winning at my rich dad's game. That is when my real education began.

I decided to follow in my rich dad's footsteps as an entrepreneur and real estate investor. I knew I had a better chance in those areas because most A students are employees, looking for high-paying jobs and investing in paper assets such as stocks, bonds, and mutual funds. Since I was a C student, I realized that I needed to use all three of my brains, not just my left brain, if I wanted to learn to win.

The questions for you are:

- What is your measurement of success?

- Where do you have the best chance of winning?

- Is your brain being trained to win?

- Are your brains working together or are they working against you?

Two Disadvantages

Over the years, I discovered that there were two disadvantages people had when it came to money. They are:

1. Our schools do not teach much about money. Even an A student leaves school knowing very little. On top of that, via the recently discovered science of mirror neurons, most of us learn about money from people who also are not financially intelligent. This is why so many people have middle-class aspirations, i.e., living below your means, saving money, and staying out of debt.

2. Our schools do not strengthen the subconscious mind. In fact, rather than educate, schools depend on fear to motivate, threaten rather than teach, imitate rather than innovate, punish mistakes rather than encourage, play it safe rather than think bigger, and say what a person wants to hear rather than what a person needs to hear.

Due to these two factors, many people *buy* when they should *sell*, *save* when they should *spend*, *spend* when they should *save*, are *fearful* when they should be *brave*, and are *brave* when they should be *fearful*.

Examples of such noncontrolled, irrational, financially foolish, subconscious brain behaviors are:

1. All the quant funds' selling at the same time, crashing the market because they were all invested in the same stocks. They were selling when they should have been buying. Panic comes from the subconscious brain. Copying or mimicking comes from the fear of being different, so they do the same thing instead of being creative and risking thinking differently.

2. When people receive a raise or come into some money, they often spend it because they feel good, instead of paying off bad debt. I know of a gentleman who inherited nearly a million dollars from his parents. Immediately he bought a big house and two new cars on credit. Instead of getting *out* of bad debt, his elation

got him into greater debt. Today he is out of money and trying to save his house.

3. When the economy turns down, the "Sales Prevention Department" of many businesses takes control. When sales drop, most business cut back on advertising, promotion, and sales staff. Rather than *save*, a business needs to *spend*. In a bad economy, the business needs to spend more on advertising and promotions, hire more sales reps, offer more sales incentives, and be more creative. In other words, be more right-brained, and communicate more. Instead of the Sales Acquisition Department taking the lead, the Sales Prevention Department takes over. The Sales Prevention Department of most companies is made up of left-brained people such as accountants, attorneys, and salaried employees, generally people with strong left brains but terrified subconscious brains. When the Sales Prevention Department takes over, many employees lose their jobs. In my opinion, when times are tough, it is the Sales Prevention Department that should shed a few employees.

The subconscious brain thinks it's intelligent. The problem with the subconscious brain is that it can be your greatest friend or your worst enemy. It takes a person with higher intelligence to step back and objectively determine which brain is talking . . . the friend or the enemy. When it comes to highly emotional subjects such as money, sex, religion, and politics, it requires a highly evolved intellect to be able to detach, expand, listen objectively, and then think clearly with both left and right brains. The problem with the subconscious brain is it's reactive, not intelligent, and not able to weigh pros and cons.

Arguing with an Idiot

It is impossible to be logical with a person speaking from his or her subconscious brain because the subconscious brain isn't logical. It can't think. It can only react. The problem is, when people are speaking via their subconscious brain they still think they are being logical and intelligent. For example, when I suggest that a businessperson spend instead of save during a recession, in most cases the subconscious brain takes over and begins giving the businessperson the logical reasons why he or she needs to cut back, to lay off employees, and to go into a money-saving mode. To most businesspeople this is logical and intelligent. They do not want to learn more. Their mind is made up. The brain is closed to new ideas.

If you push the issue, the mind becomes defensive. The walls go up, and instead of fleeing, they want to fight. They want to defend their decision and be right. Instead of learning, they become idiots. The problem with arguing with an idiot is that there are soon two idiots: you and the person you're arguing with.

One of the reasons poor people remain poor is because they have a poor person's subconscious mind. When I talk to people who are struggling financially, many will defend their right to be poor. They say such things as, "I'd rather be happy than rich," or "You have to be a crook to be rich." If you argue with them in an attempt to open their minds to new ideas, their subconscious brain often becomes more closed, more self-righteous. Soon there are two idiots having a friendly argument.

A similar event occurs with many employees and high-paid executives who like their job but want to do something else. Instead of doing what they want, their subconscious mind comes up with logical and reasonable reasons why they cannot. When informed about the high taxes they are paying as high-paid employees, they may reply, "Well, you have to pay taxes." If pressed and informed about better investments, higher returns, and less in taxes, they may reply, "That sounds risky." They close their mind to new possibilities because of fear. If you argue, there are again two idiots.

To Change Your Life . . . Change Your Environment

In my research on education and how we learn, it became very clear that environment was the most powerful teacher of all. This is why the latest validation by neuroscientists discovering mirror neurons in the brain is so important. Science is finally finding out what many of us already knew; to change your life, first change your approach.

Most of us know that if we want to lose weight, we have a better chance of success by going to a gym rather than going to a restaurant. If we want to study, it might be better to study in the quiet of a library rather than trying to read while driving a car (which I have seen people doing). If we want to relax, we leave work and go to the beach or climb a mountain. And if you want to become rich, you need to find an environment that is conducive to becoming richer, an environment that strengthens all three brains. Ironically, work and school are not those environments for most people.

The Power of Environments

If you want to grow richer and more successful, it becomes critical that you find an environment that allows all three of your brains to grow and gives them the time to develop.

By 1974, I realized that I would never be hired to work for an A student. For example, a doctor or a lawyer would never hire me because doctors and lawyers need academically and professionally smart people around them. A doctor does not want a clumsy nurse nor does a lawyer want an incompetent paralegal.

Since I was a C student, I needed to find a way to get A students to work for me. That is when I decided to be like my rich dad and become an entrepreneur and real estate investor and not like my poor dad, who was an A student and a school-teacher. I chose to become an entrepreneur and real estate investor because I am a slow learner and I knew I needed time to develop. I was not looking to become rich quickly. I was looking for an environment that suited me, where I could spend a lot of time learning slowly.

Another important reason for being an entrepreneur was that I could surround myself with smart people. I know I am not linguistic or mathematical, so I need these people as part of my team. I am still an average writer, average at math, and terrible with details. When it came to sports I knew I was better at team sports such as football, rugby, and rowing. I am not good at individual sports such as golf or tennis. Knowing this about myself, it seemed more logical for me to surround myself with smart people who also liked being on a team.

I found out the hard way that many smart people are not good on teams, which is why they excelled at school, taking tests on their own. In my world of business, I take tests every day, but not as an individual. In my world of business, I take my tests and solve my problems with a team of smart people. In other words, my genius comes out on a team. For others, such as Tiger Woods, genius comes out through the individual. The question is, are you better off as an individual or on a team?

Do It Your Way

This does not mean I am saying that you need to be an entrepreneur or real estate investor. I'm not telling you to do what I do. What I am saying is that you may want to consider a learning environment that improves your chances of winning financially. Find your own environment and your own way to financial success. For example, if you think you can become a pro golfer then you obviously need to spend much more time at the golf course engaging the mirror neurons in your brain to learn with the best golfers you can find.

The reason the discovery of mirror neurons in the brain is significant to me is because ever since 1974 I have spent most of my time with entrepreneurs and real estate investors. I am constantly seeking opportunities to do business with great entrepreneurs and real estate investors. This is why writing a book with Donald Trump in 2006 was so important to me. More than the book, it was a great opportunity to learn via mirror neurons by spending time with a great man. Spending time with him took my perspective on business, life, and standards of living to a whole new level . . . almost as much as crossing the bridge to my rich friends' homes when I was nine years old.

Finding Your Environment

Today, many business schools ask me to come and speak to their entrepreneurship classes. A common question the students ask related to financial intelligence #1: making more money, is, "How do I find investors?" or "How do I raise capital?" I understand the question because it was a question that haunted me when I left the security of Xerox and became an entrepreneur. I had no money and no one wanted to invest with me. The big venture capital firms were not knocking on my door.

My answer to the business school students is, "You just do it. You do it because you have to do it. If you don't do it you are out of business. Today, even though I have enough money, all I do is raise capital. That is all my friend Donald Trump does. His job is to raise capital. That is job number one of an entrepreneur. As entrepreneurs we raise capital from three groups of people. They are your customers, investors, and employees. Your job as an entrepreneur is to get your customers to buy your products. If you can get customers to give you money by buying your products, your investors will give you lots of money. And if you have employees, your job is to get them to produce and make at least ten times more money than you pay them. If you cannot get your employees to produce at least ten times more than you pay them, you are out of business, and if you are out of business, you do not need to raise any more money."

Obviously, this is not the answer most MBA students are looking for. Most are looking for the magic formula, the secret recipe, the quick business plan to riches. Many business school instructors squirm because most of them teach entrepreneurship, but are not entrepreneurs. Most still need a steady job, a paycheck, and are hoping for tenure. Again, it is the effect of our brains' mirror neurons not agreeing with opposing thoughts that causes them to squirm. Many business schools would rather bring in CEOs to lecture who are employees rather than entrepreneurs.

The Eyes Tell the Truth

While sharing my views on what it takes to raise capital, I watch the students' eyes. In 70 to 90 percent of them I see fear. Their eyes become glassy and their breathing becomes shallow. Blood has flowed from the left and right brains and into the primitive brain, the oldest part of the subconscious brain. Conversely, about 10 percent of the class chuckle and smile. They like my answer. Their eyes become brighter and they become excited. They know they can win. They know they can beat their classmates. They know they can become entrepreneurs. Despite an environment that thrives on fear of failure, all three of their brains are firing in alignment.

Developing the Three Parts of the Brain

For those of you who have played my *CASHFLOW* game, you may recall that to win the game requires a lot of left-brain financial knowledge and right-brain creativity. Since it is only a game, being played with fake money, the fear of failing or losing money is greatly reduced, leaving the subconscious mind more or less neutral. Once a person understands the game, the subconscious brain shifts from fear to excitement and the joy of winning. Learning becomes fun and exciting. All three brains are being educated and developing. New possibilities are opening for an expanded whole brain.

The Cone of Learning

In 2005, Arizona State University did a study on the viability of my game for teaching accounting and investing to business school students. Their findings were extremely positive and favorable, concluding that students actually learned faster and retained knowledge longer than when they learned in other ways.

The university also introduced me to the Cone of Learning, pictured on the next page.

The Second Best Way to Learn

As you can tell from the chart on page 214, the worst way to learn is by reading and the second worst way is by hearing a lecture . . . the most popular ways to teach in traditional schools. At the top of the cone is doing the real thing. When I told the MBA students to just go out and do it, many froze. Obviously there is a gap between reading, lecture, and surviving in the real world.

The Arizona State University study pointed out that just below real life is *simulations or games.* The study confirmed the Cone of Learning and that our game was the second best way to learn about the left-brained logic combined with the

The Cone of Learning

After two weeks we tend to remember		Nature of involvement
90% of what we say and do	Doing the real thing	Active
	Simulating the real experience	
	Doing a dramatic presentation	
70% of what we say	Giving a talk	
	Participating in a discussion	
50% of what we hear and see	Seeing it done on location	Passive
	Watching a demonstration	
	Looking at an exhibit Watching a demonstration	
	Watching a movie	
30% of what we see	Looking at pictures	
20% of what we hear	Hearing words	
10% of what we read	Reading	

From *Audio-Visual Methods in Teaching* 3rd edition by Dale, 1969. Reprinted with permission of Wadsworth, a division of Thomson Learning: www.thomsonrights.com. Fax 800-730-2215.

right-brained creativity of money management, accounting, and investing. Instead of being subconsciously fearful, learning was fun and motivating. Students felt more self-confidence, more empowered, eager to learn more, and better able to use what they had learned.

The university's findings were consistent with my findings as an educational entrepreneur. I found that by focusing on

Howard Gardner's fourth intelligence, bodily-kinesthetic, students learned more, learned faster, had more fun, and retained the information longer. Instead of just lectures, we played different games to make different points. I encouraged playing and making mistakes, and then we debriefed once the game was over.

The learning was powerful because games involve all three brains. Many times, participants became upset, angry, or sad. They did not like the mistakes they made. Some blamed the game or other participants. These emotions are all part of the learning process, in my classes and in real life. My job as the instructor was to guide the participant away from blame and emotions and into learning the lesson the game was teaching. Once participants got their personal lessons from the game, some broke out laughing, saying, "I didn't realize I do the same thing in real life." Once there is cognition, a relationship between behavior in the game and behavior in real life, the participant has the opportunity to make changes if he or she wants to. At that moment of cognition, the *aha!* of life, all three brains are working together. Once that occurs, the participant is often open to learning more and growing.

One great success story occurred recently at a Boys and Girls Club in a very poor part of Phoenix. A team from my company set up a CASHFLOW Club. Once again, teaching financial intelligence via a game was powerful, profound, and life-changing. One particular participant was a student who was labeled learning disabled by the school system and placed in a class for slow learners. After playing the *CASHFLOW* game a number of times with his friends, he slowly began to improve his reading and math skills. Today, he's in a regular class. This is the power of coordinating all three parts of the brain in a cooperative, peer-to-peer learning environment.

Change Your Environment . . . Change Your Life

As an educational entrepreneur, it became apparent to me that environment was the strongest teacher of all. I realized that I could teach and inform, yet if the participant went back to the same environment as before, the effect of what I taught was diminished. In other words, if the person went back to the job where mistakes were punished and creativity was suppressed, what I had taught him or her was of little value. The old environment won.

There is an old proverb that goes, "If I knew where I was going to die . . . I would not go there." Today, I know there are millions of people in environments that are not the best for their learning, wealth, and personal development. Their work and home environments are not increasing their financial intelligence and wealth. Instead of becoming richer, they become prisoners of their offices and their homes. Instead of seeking success, most people live in environments that reward playing it safe, not making mistakes, but as Paul Tudor Jones says, "One learns from mistakes, not successes."

Finding Your Genius

For people to develop their genius, they need to find the environment that supports the development of their genius. For example, Tiger Woods's environment is the golf course. He would not have done well as a jockey. Donald Trump found his strength in the tough world of New York real estate. That environment challenged him, taught him a lot, and developed his skills.

This is not an easy process. As you know, Tiger Woods works very hard at being a golf genius. Donald Trump works very hard at being a genius at real estate development. If you have ever seen the buildings he has developed in Manhattan and around the world, you know that it is easy to see his drive. Oprah survives and thrives in the very tough environment of television.

One of the reasons many people do not develop their genius is simply because they are lazy. Many just go to work to collect a paycheck. It is easier for them to be average than to work hard at developing their genius.

My questions to you are, "What do you think your genius *is* and what environment is best for you to develop it?" Another important question is, "Do you have the courage to change environments?" Imagine your future . . . if you did.

For many people the answers to these questions are "I don't know," or simply "No." For most people being comfortable is more important than finding and developing their genius. It is far easier to be average, work hard, collect a paycheck, save money, diversify in mutual funds, and live below their means. If this is you, then keep doing what you are doing.

Every one of us is different. We all have different strengths and weaknesses. This is why I do not recommend that everyone do what I did. Even though it is pretty easy to be an entrepreneur, I know that being a rich entrepreneur is not easy. The world is filled with entrepreneurs who are average. The same is true with real estate. The world is filled with real estate investors who do not make much money.

My point is this: we all have a unique talent or genius. If people want to become rich, maybe even super-rich, they need to find an environment that allows them to develop and apply their genius. This is not easy, but it can be done if you are dedicated and have the drive to win. In the real world dedication and drive are more valuable than good grades.

Environments That Make You Rich

If you want to become richer, it is important to continually upgrade your environment. This is why I shake my head every time some expert recommends living below your means. By living below your means you continually live in a lesser environment. As a young boy, every time I crossed the bridge to my rich friends' neighborhood, my brain was absorbing what it is like to live at a higher standard of living . . . a standard I wanted to live at. My brain was looking for ways I could achieve such a standard of living.

This does not mean running out and buying a big house, flashy cars, new clothes, and getting into piles of bad debt. What I mean is to consciously and intelligently challenge yourself to improve your standard of living by increasing your financial intelligence.

The best way to increase your financial intelligence is by first finding the environment where your genius can grow and develop. That can be as simple as going to a library and reading a book by a person you want to be like, or by looking at magazines with pictures of stately homes. The first step is to consciously begin to stimulate your mirror neurons to the standard of living and to the people you want to be like.

In Summary

Financially weak people are people who tend not to develop their intelligence. They seek easy environments and easy answers. These are people who get pushed around, pay too much in taxes, work hard, and live below their means. They may be smart, good, and academic, but without the financial development of all three brains they will most likely remain weak financially.

Success requires some degree of mental and physical toughness. If you can train your left brain to understand the subject, engage your right brain to come up with creative solutions, keep your subconscious brain excited rather than fearful, and then take action, while being willing to make mistakes and learn, you can create magic. You can develop your genius.

Chapter 10

Developing Your Financial IQ

Some Practical Applications

This book has been about developing your financial intelligences and raising your financial IQ. As I wrote earlier, you need to have the integrity of all five financial intelligences to become rich and successful. I know this is easier said than done. Developing your five intelligences is a lifelong process, one that cannot be accomplished in a day or even a year. I am continually working on developing my intelligences, and I encourage you to do so as well. This chapter provides some practical ways to hone your financial IQ.

Many financial advisors recommend investing for the long term. Most of them really mean for you to turn your money over to them so they can collect commissions for the long term. The problem with this advice is that you do not learn much, if anything at all. At the end of the long term, you are not necessarily financially smarter, and you have not developed your financial IQ. On top of that, most long-term investors invest in high-risk investments that offer low returns and very little control.

Instead of blindly following your financial advisor's advice, you may want to consider investing in long-term transitional environments that strengthen all three brains and provide opportunities to strengthen your financial IQ. You should look for transitional environments that will develop all three of your brains and your genius in a practical way. Some examples of transitional environments are:

1. School. School is a transitional environment for most people. Taking classes is a great way to improve left- and right-brain functions. The problem with traditional schools is that they are not environments for developing the subconscious brain, the most powerful of the three brains. Most traditional schools magnify the mirror neurons of the fear of failing and the fear of making mistakes.

2. Church. I have noticed that there are two kinds of churches: churches that teach the *love* of God and churches that teach the *fear* of God. I do not know how effective fearing God can be, yet I think church is a great place to find spiritual strength, which strengthens the subconscious brain. Hopefully with greater spiritual strength, a person will be better able to be more ethical, moral, and generous.

3. The military. The Marine Corps was a great environment for me to develop all three brains. Being a pilot required all three brains and all seven intelligences, even musical intelligence. Often, we played rock and roll music to boost our courage as we flew into combat. Today, I believe I am a better entrepreneur, especially when losing money, because I learned to improve my intrapersonal intelligence and keep my fears under control.

4. Network marketing. Most network marketing companies are incredible learning environments because they offer training, support, business structure, and products—so you can focus on developing your sales skills and building your business. I recommend that anyone who wants to be an entrepreneur join a network marketing company for some of the best real-world, street-smart business training. These companies focus on developing all three brains, and especially strengthening the subconscious brain.

Network marketing training programs are great for developing your interpersonal intelligence and your intrapersonal intelligence. Developing those two intelligences will change your life and increase your standard of living because they teach you to overcome the fear of other people and the fear of failing. The best thing about learning in the network marketing environment is that it is a supportive environment, not a fear-driven one as are schools and businesses. Instead of flunking you or firing you for below-average performance, most network marketing businesses will work to strengthen you for as long as you are willing to learn and grow. I know a number of people who spent five years with a network marketing business before finally breaking through their doubts and fears. Once they did that, the money poured in.

5. Business. There are basically two kinds of businesses . . . big and small. Big business can be a great place to develop all three brains, especially your subconscious brain. The pressure my friends in these big corporations handle is enormous. How they do it, I do not know. The mind games and back-office politics offer great opportunities to train your interpersonal and intrapersonal intelligences.

For people who want to be entrepreneurs, taking a job

with a small company can be a great learning environment. One advantage a small company has over a big company is that you can learn about all the different aspects of business. In my book *Before You Quit Your Job*, I describe the eight essential parts to a business. By working in a small business, you have a better opportunity to learn all eight and gain essential business experience.

6. Seminars. Traditional schools are important for people who want to become licensed professionals such as doctors, lawyers, and architects. They are also important for people who want to climb the corporate or government ladders where degrees from traditional accredited schools are required for promotions. Seminars, however, are great for people who want to be entrepreneurs or investors. Today there are seminars and conventions for every subject on earth. All you have to do is find the one that piques your interest.

The Rich Dad Company has excellent seminars for people who want to become real estate professionals or learn to trade stocks. I am very proud of these programs because they are taught by instructors who practice what they teach. The more advanced courses are hands-on and learning is step-by-step. For example, you will go into neighborhoods and make real offers with real money. If you are in the land development course, you will work on actual land development projects. Most importantly, our courses are designed to educate and strengthen all three brains and have them work in unison. By focusing all three brains, your profits and chances of success improve.

If you would like more information on our programs, simply go to Richdad.com and take a few minutes to find what you need.

7. Coaching. Donald Trump and I were fortunate to have rich dads who were our coaches. For anyone who has ever played a team sport, you know how important a coach can be for a team's success.

The Rich Dad Company also has a coaching division. It is staffed by professional coaches, who are not only great coaches but also practice what they coach. Rich Dad Coaching is for people who want one-on-one attention. If you would like more information on our coaching program, please go to Richdad.com. As with all Rich Dad programs, a strong emphasis is put on educating all three brains.

Now, if you are saying to yourself, "How can I afford a coach? I don't have any money," or "Why do I need a coach? I'm perfect already," think about this: when someone says, "I can't afford it," or "I don't need help," when he or she really does, it is the subconscious mind talking. This is exactly why the person needs a coach.

A coach is essential for anyone who is ready to transition from point A to point B, from one environment to the next. If not for my rich dad's coaching me for nearly thirty years, I would not be where I am today. Even today, I continue to have a number of coaches because I still have a subconscious mind that is not totally in alignment with my spirit.

8. *CASHFLOW Clubs.* Today, there are thousands of CASH-FLOW Clubs all over the world. These club leaders are volunteers who love creating a Rich Dad learning environment. Some clubs offer my Official Rich Dad 10-Step Curriculum for those who want to increase their financial intelligence. Many clubs operate for free; a few charge a nominal fee to cover expenses. For more information, go to Richdad.com and look for a CASHFLOW Club near you. Joining a club is a great way to meet like-minded people and activate the mirror neurons in your brain. You may also want to start your own CASHFLOW Club in your neighborhood, business, or church.

9. A *download for you.* On September 6, 2007, I did a video interview with Dr. Michael Carlton, MD, an expert on the brain and addictions. The title of the talk was "Can People Be Addicted to Being Poor?" It was one of the best interviews I've ever had the pleasure of being a part of. In his talk, Dr. Carlton went into greater detail on how the brain works, and why some people are rich and some are poor. It is a matter of addictions. You may have your own copy of his talk by going to Richdad.com and downloading it. I believe you will find his talk funny and extremely informative. This is our way of saying thank you to you for reading this book.

These are examples of possible transitional environments. For me, the Marine Corps, Xerox, my own businesses, and real estate investing were where I learned to develop my genius. If you want to develop your genius, what environment is best for you?

What Does It Take to Be an Entrepreneur?

Most of us know that entrepreneurs are the richest people on earth. Some of the more famous entrepreneurs today are Richard Branson, Donald Trump, Oprah Winfrey, Steve Jobs, and Rupert Murdoch.

There is an ongoing debate that asks, "Are entrepreneurs born or can entrepreneurs be developed?" The question is raised because some people think it takes a special person or a certain magic to be an entrepreneur. To me, being an entrepreneur is not that big a deal. For example, there is a junior high school girl in my neighborhood who has a thriving babysitting business and hires classmates to work for her. She is an entrepreneur. Another young boy has a handyman business after school. He is an entrepreneur. What most kids have is no fear. For most adults, that's all they have.

Two Characteristics of Entrepreneurs

Today, there are millions of people who dream of quitting their job and become entrepreneurs, running their own business. The problem is, for most people, their dream is just a dream. It never becomes a reality. So the question is, why do so many fail to go for their dream of becoming an entrepreneur?

The best answer to this age-old question comes from a friend of mine. He says, "Entrepreneurs have two characteristics . . . *ignorance* and *courage*."

This simple assessment is profound. It explains so much more than just entrepreneurship. It explains why some people are rich and why most are not. For example, one of the reasons so many A students are not rich is because they may be smart but they lack courage. There are many people who lack both knowledge and courage.

A Tale of Two Hairstylists

I have a friend who is a brilliant hairstylist. When it comes to making women look beautiful, he is a magician. For years, he's talked about opening his own salon. He has big plans, but sadly, he still remains small, running a single chair in a large salon, constantly at odds with the owner.

Another friend has a wife who became tired of being a flight attendant. Two years ago she quit her job and went to school to become a hairstylist. A month ago, she had a grand opening for her salon. It is a spectacular environment and she has attracted some of the best hairstylists to work there.

When my older friend heard about her salon, he said, "How can she open a salon? She has no talent. She is not gifted. She wasn't trained in New York like I was. And besides, she doesn't have any experience. I give her a year and she's going to fail."

She might fail. Statistics show that 90 percent of all businesses fail in the first five years. But the point of the story is the impact of *ignorance* and *courage* upon our lives. In this example, we have one hairstylist who is gifted but who lacks courage—and another hairstylist who lacks experience but has courage. In my opinion, it is this relationship between ignorance and courage that is the essence of life itself.

In 1974, I didn't have a job, money, or much business experience. I couldn't live below my means because I didn't have any means to live below. I couldn't diversify because I had nothing to diversify. All I had was courage. In the real world, *courage* is more important than good *grades. It takes courage to discover, develop, and donate your genius to the world.*

Always remember that your mind is *infinite* and your doubts are *limiting.* Ayn Rand, the author of *Atlas Shrugged*, said, "Wealth is the product of man's capacity to think." So if you are ready to change your life, find the environment that will allow all three of your brains to think and grow richer. And who knows, you might find your genius.

Your Feedback Loop: No Man Is an Island

We live in a world of feedback. When we climb on a bathroom scale, our weight is giving us feedback. If the scale says we are ten pounds heavier, we may not like the feedback, especially if we are already twenty pounds overweight. When your doctor takes your blood pressure and sends your blood sample to a lab, your doctor is looking for feedback.

Feedback is important. It can be a very important source of information about us and our environment. The problem is, if we do not like the feedback, our subconscious minds may block out, distort, diminish, or deny the importance of the information coming from feedback.

One of the most enlightening lessons I learned from the Marine Corps was the importance of feedback. When I was messing up the feedback was pretty intense and definitely not sugar-coated. When I worked with my rich dad, there was the same intensity of feedback. In doing our book together, I received very fast and blunt feedback from Donald Trump. If not for my military training, or working with my rich dad, I know I never could have worked with Donald. His feedback was quick, to the point, and direct. I know that if I had argued back, disagreed, or not listened to Donald's feedback, I would not be working with him—nor would I have learned as much.

I mention this because today many of us work in environments where feedback is not allowed, not forthright, and not honest. Many schools and businesses are afraid to tell you what you need to hear for fear of being sued. Many friends and co-workers will speak behind your back because they lack the courage to speak to your face. This is not a healthy environment. It is a dysfunctional environment.

A healthy environment is one that offers feedback. Life is constantly giving you priceless information if you are willing to receive it, and most of the time the feedback is free. Every time you open your pay envelope and see how much is lost to taxes, this is feedback. If your creditors are calling, demanding payment, this is feedback. If you are working harder and not earning enough, this is feedback. If you are spending more time at work and less time at home, this is feedback. If your kids are on drugs and being chased by the law, this is feedback. If your friends are all losers and like being losers, this is feedback. It is great information. The real world is trying to tell you something.

Your standard of living is a great source of feedback. If you are living in a home that makes you feel poor, that is feedback. If you are driving a cheap car when you would rather be driving a Lamborghini, that is feedback. Standard of living is simply the standard you feel most at home with. It does not mean being comfortable, cheap, or compromising. Standard of living means you are in love with and proud of your home, friends, and possessions rather than envying someone else's standard of living. Again, this does not mean improving your standard by getting into debt. I'm talking about improving your standard of living by first finding a great environment to learn, getting smarter, and then growing richer.

You do not need to go to a great school, have a great job, or read great books to receive some of the best information in the world. All you have to do is look at the world around you and listen to the feedback.

There are three important things to know about feedback:

1. Have the courage to be open to feedback. If you want to improve, seek more feedback. This is why coaches and mentors are important to successful people. Successful people seek more feedback.

2. Offer feedback or advice only if it's asked for. Nothing infuriates people more than feedback they did not ask for . . . even if it's feedback they know they need. As that ancient bit of wisdom goes, "Don't teach pigs to sing. It wastes your time and it annoys the pig."

3. Con men will tell you what you want to hear rather than tell you what you need to hear. Con men prey on the mentally uninformed and emotionally weak. They will tune in to where you are weak, and then they will craft a marketing message that matches that weakness. In the world of money, con men have gotten the masses to believe that diversification and living below your means is smart, even though the smartest investors such as Warren Buffett do not diversify and do not recommend living below your means.

Buffett lives at *his* standard of living, which is very different than Donald Trump's standard of living. Warren Buffett lives in Omaha, Nebraska, and Donald Trump lives in New York City. The point is, both men have the means to live anywhere in the world and at any standard of living they want to live at. They are happy where they are.

More important questions are:

- Are you living where you want to live and at the standard of living you want to live at?

- Are you diversifying and living below your means so that con men can live above their means?

- Are you associating with friends and people you want to be associated with?

If you want to become healthier, smarter, richer, and happier, pay closer attention to your own feedback. It is offering you the most important information in the world. Regardless of whether you like your feedback or not, if you have the courage to listen to it and learn from it, you will succeed. Thank you for reading this book.

Afterword: The License to Print Money

When I began writing this book in 2007, the housing and credit crises were just beginning to emerge as a major problem. At the time it was not certain just how far-reaching the problem would be. And while I was not certain how much havoc the crisis would cause in the financial markets, I was certain of one thing: *The middle class would suffer.*

I knew that those who lived by the old rules of money such as *work hard, save money, get out of debt, and invest for the long term in a well-diversified portfolio of stocks, bonds, and mutual funds*, were the ones who would suffer the most. They would stand by and watch in silent desperation as the values of their homes and retirement accounts drastically dropped, as they went from perceived financial stability to the brink of financial ruin.

A Year Later But Not a Year Smarter

A lot has changed in the last year, and as I write this afterword in August 2008, it is clear that housing and credit crises have drastically affected the financial markets and consequently the entire U.S. economy. Today, housing prices are falling at a record pace. The U.S. stock market is officially in bear territory, having dropped more than 20 percent from its high. Inflation is at a twenty-six-year high and gasoline is above four dollars a gallon. The U.S. is nearing, or already in, what many consider to be a long and painful recession. You don't need me to tell you this. The bad news is on the front page of every major news source.

Though many aspects have changed in the economy since I first wrote *Increase Your Financial IQ*, one facet has not changed—the basic premise of the book. I wrote this book because I know that the rules of money drastically changed in 1971:

- In 1971, President Nixon took the U.S. off the gold standard.

- In 1971, the U.S. granted itself the license to print money.

These fundamental changes in the way money works are the root of our economic problems today. They are also the reason why the rich keep getting richer and the poor keep getting poorer—and why the middle class is slowly being wiped out.

As you know by now, the premise of *Increase Your Financial IQ* is simply this:

It is not money, but knowledge that makes you rich.

A person with a high financial IQ and financial intelligence has a lot of knowledge about money. As I've said, financial intelligence is not the most important form of intelligence, but it is an essential one. You will not be able to survive and thrive financially in today's economy without a high financial IQ and a deep understanding about how the rules of money have changed.

Unfortunately, our educational system in America is broken. Our teachers force feed our children a lot of facts, and then train them through a fear of failure to regurgitate those facts. But our educational system does not train our children to solve problems. And it especially doesn't teach them how to solve money problems or give students knowledge of how money works. At the most it teaches them to balance a checkbook and gives them a brief overview of the old rules of money, teaching them to save money and invest in mutual funds.

The Middle Class Is a Loser

I do not mean to insult the middle class. But the fact remains that the middle class is a loser in today's economy because the educational system has failed it. Because those in the middle class do not know how money works and that the rules of money have changed, they continue to struggle financially, holding on to the old rules of money, desperately hoping that those rules will save them. In turn, they teach their children the same old rules of money because it is all they know. All the while they become poorer and their children become poorer.

The Rich Are Winners

In contrast, the rich do not obey the old rules of money. They have a deep understanding and a vast knowledge of how money works—and how to make money work for them. The rich know that the rules of money have changed, and they use those rules to their advantage to create money out of thin air just by using their financial intelligence. The rich also teach their children that the old rules of money are dead. They teach their children how to make money work for *them*, not the other way around. Consequently, they and their children become richer and richer. The rich are winners in today's economy.

Knowledge: The License to Print Money

But no matter how much money the rich have, it is not their money that makes them rich or their children rich. Rather it is their *knowledge* about how money works that makes them rich. Their knowledge is an asset they use to create money out of thin air. In a very real sense, through their knowledge of how money works, the rich have a license to print money—legally.

The gap between those who work for money and those with a license to print money is one reason why there is such a gap between the rich and everyone else. I had two educations when it came to money. My poor dad taught me the middle-class mind-set, and my rich dad taught me the mind-set of the rich. My poor dad worked for money, and my rich dad taught me to legally print money.

What Is Money?

You might be thinking to yourself that I've finally gone off my rocker. That is, how can I possibly claim I have figured out how to print money legally? The reason many people find this concept hard to grasp is because they have a fundamental misunderstanding of what money is. So let me provide a brief overview of what money is in today's economy. It is also an explanation of why financial intelligence is more important today than it has ever been. Today, your financial IQ is your real money. (For a fuller explanation on money and the evolution of money I recommend you read my friend Mike Maloney's book, *Rich Dad's Guide to Investing in Gold and Silver,* and Richard Duncan's book, *The Dollar Crisis.*)

The following is a brief history of the *evolution of money*.

BARTER

Before there was money, there was barter. For example, if I grew tomatoes and wanted eggs, I could trade two tomatoes for two eggs with a chicken farmer. Barter was efficient as long as I could trade my tomatoes for the things I needed. But if no one wanted tomatoes, I starved.

COMMODITIES

As humans became more civilized, barter was no longer an efficient way of trading. Early forms of money were shells, beads, colored rocks, arrowheads, and whatever else people agreed upon as symbols of value. For example, if I did not need two eggs, I could give the chicken farmer two tomatoes, and he would give me two shells, rather than two eggs, so I could trade the shells with someone who had what I wanted.

For thousands of years, people who had access to gold and silver valued these precious metals for use as money in this way. Gold and silver have intrinsic value, which means they can be used for something other than money, such as jewelry. So true money had intrinsic value. True money could be accurately measured. And true money could be stored for years. Gold and silver were compact enough to be carried long distances. Tomatoes or eggs did not last long enough to retain their intrinsic value. Other things like oil have intrinsic value and are measureable, but the problem is that they aren't easily carried in your wallet.

RECEIPT MONEY

For an individual who had gold or silver, it was often safer to place it with someone who would take care of it. The individual would turn the gold or silver over to the person with a safe, and that person would issue a receipt for the gold or silver. This was one of the earliest forms of paper money. It was receipt money.

Over the years, a person would carry the receipt, rather

than gold or silver, and then buy something with the receipt. The person with the receipt could then go to the person who held the gold or silver and trade the receipt for possession of the precious metals.

As time progressed, these storage places for valuables became today's modern banks. Soon people got used to the idea of trading bank receipts rather than gold or silver. As long as people trusted the banker, people were happy to trade paper receipts.

When I was a kid, the U.S. dollar was receipt money. That means, when I looked at a dollar bill, the bill would say, "One dollar payable to the bearer on demand." That meant there was a dollar's worth of silver backing the paper U.S. dollar. Today, the U.S. dollar says, "In God We Trust," and the U.S. Treasury says this about its value: "The notes have no value for themselves, but for what they will buy." In another sense, because they are legal tender, Federal Reserve notes are "backed" by all the goods and services in the economy. And as we know, the "goods and services" of the U.S. economy are quickly diminishing in value.

FRACTIONAL RESERVES

The bankers soon realized that very few people ever redeemed their receipts for the gold or silver. It soon became obvious to the bankers that they could write more receipts for the gold and silver in storage. It was not long before the bankers were issuing more and more receipts. As long as people thought their gold and silver were safe, things were fine. However, if people ever lost confidence in the banks or the banks' notes, there would be a run on the bank in which people would rush to withdraw their gold and silver. If the bank did not have enough reserves on hand to cover the withdrawals, it would collapse. This happened most dramatically during the Great Depression. And it happened most recently with the collapse of Indy Mac, one of the largest banking failures in U.S. history.

Today, it is estimated that, for every dollar in savings, the bank will lend out twenty dollars. The system is thus called a fractional reserve system because the banks only need a fraction of the dollars they lend out to actually be in their possession, in this case $1/20^{th}$. On top of that, the banker might pay you 5 percent interest on your dollar (if you're lucky) but can charge up to 20 percent interest to the person who borrows the twenty dollars. Over the course of a year, the banks pay you five cents on your dollar, and they make four dollars (20% × $20) on your one dollar. That is why owning a bank is so profitable—that is unless you make foolish loans like banks such as Indy Mac did that led up to the current housing and credit crisis.

FIAT MONEY

Today, the U.S. system of money is purely fiat. A fiat is simply a decree or arbitrary command. Thus, fiat money is money that a government creates by decree without anything backing it up, other than reputation of the government itself. It is man-made money with no intrinsic value. The U.S. Bureau of Engraving, which prints our money, is working around the clock, using eighteen tons of ink each month, merely printing money. Yet the U.S. dollar has no intrinsic value and, because it is based upon debt, it actually is worth less than nothing. In actuality, it is a liability. The government creates laws that force you to accept this man-made money. If you do not accept it, you can be punished. Fiat money is technically counterfeit money that is backed by laws.

In 1971, when President Nixon took the U.S. off the gold standard, the U.S. government granted itself the license to print money and began an experiment in fiat money that was doomed to failure—just like every other experiment in fiat money in history.

Simply put, fiat money is imaginary money. Because it is imaginary, it is tough to visualize, and explaining the system of fiat money can be very confusing.

To make things simpler, I will use an example of a credit card to explain fiat money. When a bank sends you a credit card there is technically no money in existence to account for your credit balance. Neither is there any debt. So, if you have a credit balance of $10,000, there is no $10,000 in a bank to back it up. A credit card is just a piece of plastic with your name and some numbers on it. The moment you use your credit card, however, to pay $10 for school supplies for instance, at that moment $10 is created and $10 of debt is created. Up until that moment there was nothing. But the moment you swipe your card, fiat money is magically created.

For those of you who have read *Rich Dad Poor Dad*, you may recognize the following diagram:

Asset	Liability
$10	$10

The moment you use your credit card, you magically add $10 to the world economy. You also create a $10 liability (debt), which is a promise to pay back that same $10 to the world economy.

In today's economy, nobody wants you to pay off your debt. If you pay off your debt, money disappears. This is why credit card companies never want you to pay the money back. If you pay back the $10 in five days, the balance sheet looks like this.

Asset	Liability
$0	$0

Banks do not make money with zero dollars in their asset and liability columns. Technically, banks and credit card companies create funny money (counterfeit money), lend that funny money out, and then make money on the interest paid for that funny money, which was created out of thin air. (I know this is complicated, which is why it is so hard for most people to understand the modern banking system.)

Let's get back to your personal financial statement. What banks want you to do is spend the $10 on your credit card and never pay back the loan. They want you to pay interest forever. This is what the bank wants to see.

Your financial statement:

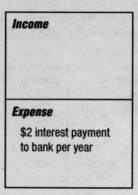

Take a moment to think about and understand that concept. Why this is difficult to understand is because the bank never really had the ten dollars. It was created out of thin air the moment you used your credit card. The bank wants you to pay the interest, in this example 20 percent, for as long as it takes you to retire the borrowed $10 (money the bank created out of thin air). In other words, modern money is only credit, a debt to be repaid. And that credit is simply moved from one source to another with nothing tangibly backing it.

The system only works as long as the borrower continues to pay the interest. Recently, however, during this subprime mortgage meltdown, the system stopped working when the subprime borrower could no longer pay the minimum payments. When the borrower stopped paying, the whole credit system of the world backed up like a toilet. Unfortunately, this problem has been backing up in the sewer pipes since 1971.

The Credit Crisis

Today, the world shakes in terror because the bankers are in deep trouble. The bankers are unable to pay back their own loans to other banks. If the banks do not make loans or cannot pay back their loans, the economy starts to collapse and people suffer. That is because 75 percent of our economic growth is a result of consumer spending. And since we currently have the worst savings rate in the history of the United States, we have no other way to spend than to borrow money. If credit dries up—that is, if the banks stop lending money or make it much harder to qualify for credit—he U.S. consumer will not be able to spend. If consumers stop spending, the economy will suffer greatly. The only way for the economy to grow is for us to begin to borrow once again.

For years, the Federal Reserve Bank, the World Bank, and the International Monetary Fund (IMF) have been handing out credit cards to subprime countries, subprime investors, and subprime borrowers all over the world. The credit problem today is measured in the trillions of dollars of "magic" money—money created out of thin air, hoping that people will keep paying the interest and continue to borrow more money.

We are now watching this system slowly collapse. Blinded by greed, banks and institutions lowered their standards such that they gave loans out to anyone who could make a mirror fog. When I first wrote *Increase Your Financial IQ*, very few people were talking about how large this problem had become. Now, it is all you hear about. All those loans are now being defaulted on by the very same subprime borrowers the banks were falling over themselves to service. As a result, banks are having to make huge adjustments to their asset and liability columns (write-downs) as the money they expected to receive in interest has dried up. Even worse, the things they lent the money for are now in their possession, but only at a fraction of the value they issued the loan for. As a result, banks are now afraid to loan any money out, which is dragging the whole economy down and lowering the standard of living for millions of Americans.

It is not the rich, however, who are being hurt by this phenomenon. It is the middle class. The middle class is now joining the ranks of the poor. And the rich are becoming richer because of the credit crisis. Here is what I mean.

Real Money

Today, millions of people are calling for a return to the gold standard. In other words, they want to turn the clock back to pre-1971. Saying it another way, some people, such as former presidential candidate Ron Paul, want us to go back to the time when money was commodity money.

While it is possible that this *might* happen, it is not *probable*, and the pain of doing so would probably mean a massive collapse of the entire global economic system.

But rather than wait in hopes of turning back the clock, it is the position of the Rich Dad Company that it is time for financial education. It is time to raise the financial intelligence and ultimately the financial IQ of those who want to learn the difference between assets and liabilities, and who want to know how to print their own money. In today's economy it is your knowledge, or your financial IQ, that is your real money.

The main reason people are in trouble is because they borrow money to buy liabilities, such as their homes, cars, and televisions—liabilities that cost them money every month in the form of interest—but that generate no income and quite often lose value over time. Those possessions actually make them poorer. On the other hand, people would be richer if they borrowed money to purchase assets, such as rental property or businesses that generate income.

Commodities such as gold, oil, silver, and land provided real wealth in the Industrial Age. But in the Information Age, these commodities themselves do not make you rich. Rather, it is the information you have about those commodities. Real wealth in the Information Age is your financial intelligence. Explaining further, today we all know that we can both make and lose money investing in real estate, stocks, gold, oil, and businesses. In other words, it is not the tangible asset that makes you rich. Today, real wealth is more than financial information; it is the financial intelligence to process information and turn information into personal wealth. In the Information Age, your real wealth, your real asset, is your financial IQ.

MONEY AS CURRENCY

The reason why your real asset or money is your financial IQ is that there is no such thing as real money any longer. As I talked about in the first chapter of this book, money has simply become a currency. And the easiest way to understand currency is to think of an electric current. An electric current must continually move or it will cease to exist. It is simply a means to transfer electricity from one source to another. Likewise, our money as currency must continually move from one asset to another or it, too, will die.

While it is nice to imagine that the U.S. monetary system will go back to a gold standard where our money is backed by something tangible, the reality is that our money is not backed by anything other than faith and good credit. As a nation we are losing our good credit. That is why the dollar has dropped drastically relative to other major currencies around the world.

Thus, what is of value is not our money itself, but the revenue-producing assets that money can buy us. Understanding this concept is the first step towards increasing your financial IQ.

DOUBLE-EDGED SWORDS

There are three double-edged swords in today's economy that explain why so many people are struggling financially. They are double-edged swords because, while they make most people poorer, they also can make financially smart people richer. They are:

1. Taxes
2. Interest
3. Inflation

After 1971, after the U.S. began printing money with no backing, people began paying more taxes, interest, and higher prices due to inflation.

The reasons why the rich get richer are because they pay less in taxes, they know the difference between interest on good debt versus bad debt, and inflation makes them richer. Most importantly, the rich know how to legally print money, just like the government does.

Let me explain.

Taxes

If you physically work for money, you will pay taxes. The harder you work, the more you make, and the more you pay in taxes. As you may or may not know, the U.S. tax system is a sliding scale that charges a higher percentage of your money in taxes for the more you make. Under this system, people who work hard, get promoted, and make more money are actually punished for their initiative.

Rather than working for money, the rich get richer because they have their money work for them. As I discussed throughout this book, taxes are lower on passive income from my investments and higher on earned income from my labor. For example, in America, I can pay zero percent in taxes from capital gains made from my real estate investments if I have a high financial IQ. As as of this writing, the highest tax I pay on capital gains is 20 percent. For my earned income—the money I make as an employee—I can pay as high as 50 percent in taxes. Obviously, I would rather have my money work hard for me and pay lower taxes.

Interest

In 1997 I made what was at the time a heretical statement in my book *Rich Dad Poor Dad*. I said, "Your house is not an asset." I might as well have been a witch in seventeenth-century Salem, Massachusetts. Howls of protest went up, and people demanded I be figuratively burned at the stake.

When I make that statement today, the howls of protest have mysteriously disappeared. That is because it is now easy for people to understand how a house is really a liability because it does not put money in your pocket; it only takes it out in the form of mortgage interest, maintenance, and property taxes. And now that many houses cannot even be sold for the original loan amount borrowed against them, houses have indeed become a major liability. In fact they are such a liability that a record number of people are now simply walking away from them. Perhaps you've heard of "jingle mail"? That is the phenomenon of cash-strapped homeowners mailing their keys to the lender and walking away from their homes. In the year since I wrote *Increase Your Financial IQ*, foreclosure filings are up *121 percent* and are only expected to climb.

For many people, their home is considered their biggest investment, and for many people, in the years of easy credit it was a bigger investment than they could possibly afford. Yet, many justified buying more than they could afford, saying to themselves, "Housing prices always go up." You can now see that a house is not an asset. It is a liability.

In addition, one of the reasons the rich get richer is that they know the difference between interest on good debt and bad debt. Bad debt is debt you pay for. Bad debt also makes you poorer. A mortgage on a house only makes you poorer because *you* pay the interest on that debt. Likewise, if you have car loans, school loans, and credit card loans, the interest payments take a large percentage of your income.

Good debt, on the other hand, is debt someone else pays for. Good debt makes you richer. For example, when I buy an apartment house, I may borrow millions of dollars and pay hundreds of thousands a year in interest. But the key difference is that my renters pay the mortgage payment, interest, and my operating expenses—and I receive all the income from my investment. In this example, interest on my good debt costs me nothing and truly makes me richer.

Inflation

The worst of all the double-edged swords is inflation because it is hidden. Since it is hidden, most people are unaware or have only a vague idea of how inflation steals from them, acting as a hidden tax.

Inflation is caused by the U.S. Federal Reserve Bank's license to print money, which is often a direct result of government spending. Inflation is *not* caused by prices going up. Inflation is caused by the purchasing power of your money going down. Inflation decreases the value of a person's labor and savings.

This is why it is very important to understand the concept of fiat money as currency when it comes to the new rules of money. Under the new rules, those who save their dollars are losers. The government can and will print more money and inject it into the system. Each time the government prints more money it is, in effect, "stealing" from the American citizen. That is because the amount of goods in the economy is the same, but there are now more dollars chasing them. Thus, it takes more dollars to purchase them. The simple rule is that the more dollars that are chasing a product, the higher the price will be. Gasoline at $4 a gallon is a good example of this.

As I write this, inflation is at a twenty-six-year high. The problem of inflation is only going to get worse. The government has simply given out too many promises to pay for things it doesn't have the money for. Long-standing problems have been Medicare and Social Security. These are obvious, and many people already know they are a problem for the government and future economic health.

More recent promises that many people may not fully understand are the problems of the government bailing out or financially backing major corporations like Bear Stearns, Fannie Mae, and Freddie Mac. These government actions "steal" from the American citizen in order to support major corporations. Rather than paying for their mistakes, these companies are saved by taxpayer money that does not exist. For instance, the recent housing bill passed by Congress on July 26, 2008, provides $2.25 billion dollars in credit lines to Fannie and Freddie from the U.S. Treasury. It also provides $300 billion in government-backed FHA loans to help refinance mortgages for people who are facing foreclosure. Ironically, the very same people who could not afford to pay banks their money will now be asked to pay the government even more money. When—not if—the FHA loans are foreclosed on, it will be the American taxpayer who will foot the bill. It is a losing proposition for everyone—except, of course, for the corporations that are bailed out. If you were to look at how this helps a corporation's financial statement, it would look like this: See following page.

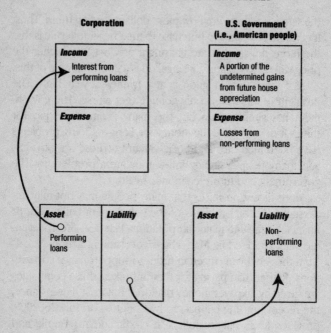

On the other hand, the U.S. government's—a.k.a. the U.S. people's—financial statement would look like this:

Income
A portion of the undetermined gains from future house appreciation

Expense
Losses from non-performing loans

Asset	Liability
	Non-performing loans

Almost lost in the discussion about the housing bill, however, is the fact that it contains a measure allowing for the government to increase the U.S. debt to $10.6 *trillion*. The reason is that the government does not have the money to pay for the housing bill programs or its bailouts of major corporations. Instead, the Fed will have to print more money to pay these debts, causing inflation to go even higher. Thus U.S. taxpayers not only pay for these programs through their tax dollars, they also pay for them through the hidden tax of inflation, which devalues the dollar. That is why saving your money is a losing proposition. Rather, you should do what the rich do and actually profit from inflation.

The rich profit from inflation by using their money to purchase assets that not only provide cash flow but also benefit from inflation. For example, when there is inflation, I can raise the rent on my real estate. If my rents go up, the value of my property goes up. Inflation also causes the replacement cost of my property, which is the difference between the price of purchasing an apartment house or building a new one, to go up. Also, as an investor in oil, I make more money each time the price of oil goes up. These are examples of inflation making me richer.

Another advantage of investing in rental real estate and oil is that I gain additional tax advantages from the government. In real estate, one major tax advantage is *depreciation*. Through depreciation I am able to deduct an IRS-determined portion of my assets value from my income on my tax return over a certain number of years. This helps me because while it is technically not a loss in that no money actually comes out of my pocket, the government nonetheless treats it as a loss on my income statement, which lowers the amount of income I have to pay taxes on. In oil, I receive tax incentives to drill for oil and another tax break when I sell oil to a refinery. When I sell oil, I receive a tax break for *depletion,* which in many ways is similar to real estate's *depreciation.*

As these examples demonstrate, taxes, interest, and inflation make most people poorer. For the financially intelligent, however, taxes, interest, and inflation can actually make them richer. Generally the difference is found in the diagram of the Cashflow Quadrant, which I explained in detail in chapter two, and which you can learn more about in my book, *Cashflow Quadrant*.

The letters in the Cashflow Quadrant stand for the following:

- E stands for Employee.
- S stands for Small Business or Specialist such as a doctor, plumber, or self-employed person.
- B stands for Big Business entrepreneurs who build companies with more than 500 employees.
- I stands for Investors.

People who are hurt by taxes, interest, and inflation are generally on the E and S side of the quadrant.

The most important reason why the rich get richer by understanding the new rules of money is explained in the next section.

The License To Print Money

As we've discussed, after 1971 the U.S was allowed to legally print money. The U.S. dollar no longer had to be backed by gold or silver.

In 1971, the U.S. Federal Reserve Bank—which is neither "U.S." nor "Federal", technically has no reserves, and is not really a bank—was given the right to print U.S. currency by the government. While the Fed doesn't have reserves, it does have a printing press. The Fed has been allowed to flood the world with dollars, also known as funny money, magic money, fiat money: currency. While this did the world some good, such as increasing the standard of living of many countries and making many people rich, it also caused many people to become poorer by not only having to work harder but ultimately earning less money. They earned less money because they paid more in taxes, interest, and inflation.

In a true capitalist system, there should be no inflation. In a true capitalist system, prices should come down and productivity should go up. For example, computers today cost less and do more. That is an example of capitalism working properly. One reason why prices go up is because inefficient socialist governments cost more and do less. And once the banks and government officials took over our money supply, it drove costs up because the purchasing power of money went down.

To beat this system of funny money, my rich dad said to me, "If the government has a license to print money, you should learn to print your own money." The following are some examples of how, in effect, I do that.

Real Estate

Early in my real estate career, when the housing market was in an upward cycle, I would use my financial IQ by buying a house for $100,000. I would immediately sell it to someone with bad credit, and who couldn't qualify for a bank loan, for $120,000, providing that person with both the house and the loan. By doing this, I instantly created $20,000 that did not exist before. In truth, I never wanted the person to pay the house off. Just like the credit card company that only wants you to make a minimum payment, all I wanted was the interest payments on the loan. If my interest rate was 10 percent, I would earn $2,000 a year in interest on the $20,000 I created out of thin air. Best of all, the new owner paid for all the expenses of maintaining the property.

As I mentioned, people who purchased this type of real estate were generally people who did not have enough money for a down payment or could not qualify for a conventional mortgage. But it was a win-win situation for me, especially when housing prices were rising due to inflation. It may not be a good idea to use this strategy in a declining real estate market. In this example, if housing prices were falling, I could lose financially if the value of the house dropped to $80,000. I only use this as an example of legally printing my own money by using real estate.

Again, this only goes to show that it is not money or even your assets that are your true wealth. Rather it is your knowledge of how money works that allows you to create money as opportunities present themselves. Economic conditions always change, but a person with a high financial IQ can become rich regardless of the situation.

Write a Book

When I write a book, I am, in effect, printing money. I write the book once and I then license the rights to publish my book to approximately sixty publishers throughout the world. Every quarter, the publishers send me a royalty payment for the number of books they sell. I have no further expenses and only pure income for years. Writing a book is a license to print money. If I sell millions of copies, I can earn millions of dollars.

Sell Shares of My Business

Another method of printing money is to build a business and sell shares in the business through an I.P.O., which stands for Initial Public Offering. These shares in a public company are usually sold through stock markets such as New York's

Wall Street, Tokyo's Nikkei, and the stock exchanges in London and Toronto.

In recent years, twentysomethings became billionaires by selling shares in their companies, such as Microsoft, Apple, and Google. These young entrepreneurs "printed their own money."

Personally, I have taken two companies public, but nothing close to, or as famous or enriching as Apple or Google. Nonetheless I learned to print money via selling shares of a business I built rather than buying or trading shares of someone else's business. A good friend of mine, who has been a venture capitalist for over fifty years, always says, "The rich don't buy stocks; they sell stocks." The rich create companies and then sell the company's shares to investors. That is legally printing money.

Franchising My Business

Rather than taking Rich Dad public, I decided to legally print money by expanding the business through a franchise system. A franchise system such as McDonalds, the most famous of all franchises, is another way to legally print money. When I franchise my business, I give entrepreneurs a license to operate under the Rich Dad brand. In return they pay me a fee and share their proceeds with Rich Dad. Watch for the Rich Dad Franchise as it rolls out throughout the world. Possibly after the Rich Dad Franchise is global, I may then take it public through an I.P.O., again legally printing more money.

One reason I like the idea of taking a company public or franchising the business is because these are ways of sharing the wealth created from my business. Not only do I make money out of thin air, but I also help entrepreneurs do the same by allowing them to capitalize on the Rich Dad brand.

Invest in Yourself: A Lifetime of Education

The purpose of this book, and of the Rich Dad Company for that matter, is not to teach you what to do to get rich. The "what to do" changes all the time. Rather, I've made it my personal mission to equip you to be financially intelligent. My goal is for you to know the new rules of money so that when an opportunity comes along for you to create money, you are smart enough to recognize it. My goal is to increase your financial IQ.

In order to become rich you must stop thinking of wealth in terms of money. Money is simply a by-product of your true wealth—your financial IQ. Many people were good at making money under the old rules of money. It was far easier to make money under those rules because all you had to do was work hard, save, and invest conservatively. Today, it is much more difficult to make money and keep it if you do not have a high financial IQ. That is why the gap between the rich and the poor is growing, not shrinking. That is why the middle class is being wiped out.

If you do not believe that the rules of money have changed, you're toast. If you still think it is smart to work hard, save your money, and invest in a well-diversified portfolio of mutual funds, you will become poorer.

Just the mere fact that you are reading this book leads me to believe that you don't think that way. I commend you on working towards increasing your financial IQ, and encourage you to form a lifelong habit of education. A financially intelligent person will always have something to learn because there is always a new problem to be solved. And as you now know, each new problem solved is a deposit in your asset column because you are increasing the true source of your wealth—your financial IQ.

I ask you to seriously reflect on chapter ten of this book. Consider what it will take for you to continue increasing your financial intelligence and furthering your knowledge of money. Surround yourself with those who are smarter than you and find as many mentors as you can. My definition of a mentor is simple: someone who is already where you want to be. Recognize that once you attain the same level of understanding and stature as your mentors you not only owe them a lifetime of gratitude, you also owe it to them to find new mentors who can help take you even further.

One of the greatest sources of education I can recommend is Rich Dad's Education, which is a partnership the Rich Dad Company has with the Whitney Information Network. Its programs are available all over the United States and are very dynamic. You will be able to find quality instruction and mentorship through its programs. It will be an essential tool in helping you to increase your financial IQ. You can find out more about Rich Dad's Education at richdadeducation.com.

In conclusion, I ask you to remember the following:

- In 1971, the rules of money changed. The old rules of working hard, saving, and investing in a well diversified portfolio of stocks, bonds, and mutual funds are dead, and they will only make you poorer.

- Dollars are now backed by nothing. Thus, your financial IQ is your true money. Your financial IQ is what will make you rich.

- Taxes, interest, and inflation can make you either poor or rich. It all depends on your financial IQ.

I guarantee that if you treat life like a learning adventure, and if you always strive to increase your financial IQ, wealth will come your way. Thank you again for reading this book, and enjoy the adventure.

Robert T. Kiyosaki

Robert Kiyosaki, author of *Rich Dad Poor Dad*—the international runaway bestseller that has held a top spot on the *New York Times* bestseller list for over six years—is an investor, entrepreneur, and educator whose perspectives on money and investing fly in the face of conventional wisdom. He has, virtually single-handedly, challenged and changed the way tens of millions around the world think about money.

Rich Dad Poor Dad is the bestselling personal finance book of all time, and has enjoyed prominence on the *BusinessWeek, Wall Street Journal,* and *USA Today* bestseller lists. It was named "*USA Today*'s #1 Money Book" two years in a row.

Translated into 51 languages and available in 109 countries, the Rich Dad series has sold over 27 million copies worldwide and has dominated bestseller lists across Asia, Australia, South America, Mexico, and Europe. In 2005, Robert was inducted into Amazon.com's Hall of Fame as one of that bookseller's Top 25 Authors. There are currently 13 books in the Rich Dad series.

Robert writes a biweekly column—"Why the Rich Are Getting Richer"—for Yahoo! Finance and a monthly column titled "Rich Returns" for *Entrepreneur* magazine.

Born and raised in Hawaii, Robert Kiyosaki is a fourth-generation Japanese-American. After graduating from college in New York, Robert joined the Marine Corps and served in Vietnam as an officer and helicopter gunship pilot. Following the war, Robert went to work in sales for Xerox Corporation and, in 1977, started a company that brought the first nylon and Velcro "surfer wallets" to market. He founded an international education company in 1985 that taught business and investing to tens of thousands of students throughout the world. In 1994 Robert sold his business and, through his investments, was able to retire at the age of 47. During his short-lived retirement he wrote *Rich Dad Poor Dad*.

Bestselling Books
by Robert T. Kiyosaki and Sharon L. Lechter

Rich Dad Poor Dad
What the Rich Teach Their Kids About Money
that the Poor and Middle Class Do Not

Rich Dad's CASHFLOW Quadrant
Rich Dad's Guide to Financial Freedom

Rich Dad's Guide to Investing
What the Rich Invest In that the Poor and Middle Class Do Not

Rich Dad's Rich Kid Smart Kid
Give Your Child a Financial Head Start

Rich Dad's Retire Young Retire Rich
How to Get Rich Quickly and Stay Rich Forever

Rich Dad's Prophecy
Why the Biggest Stock Market Crash in History is Still Coming...
And How You Can Prepare Yourself and Profit From it!

Rich Dad's Success Stories
Real-Life Success Stories from Real-Life People
Who Followed the Rich Dad Lessons

Rich Dad's Guide to Becoming Rich Without Cutting Up Your Credit Cards
Turn "Bad Debt" into "Good Debt"

Rich Dad's Who Took My Money?
Why Slow Investors Lose and Fast Money Wins!

Rich Dad Poor Dad for Teens
The Secrets About Money – That You Don't Learn In School!

Rich Dad's Escape from the Rat Race
How to Become a Rich Kid by Following Rich Dad's Advice

Rich Dad's Before You Quit Your Job
Ten Real-Life Lessons Every Entrepreneur Should Know
About Building a Multi-Million Dollar Business